Y0-BDA-614

A BROKEN SILENCE

Voices of African American Women in the Academy

LENA WRIGHT MYERS

Foreword by Essie Manuel Rutledge

Bergin & Garvey
Westport, Connecticut • London

Library of Congress Cataloging-in-Publication Data

Myers, Lena Wright.
A broken silence : voices of African American women in the academy / Lena Wright Myers ; foreword by Essie Manuel Rutledge.
p. cm.
Includes bibliographical references and index.
ISBN 0–89789–793–5 (alk. paper)
1. African American women college teachers. 2. Discrimination in higher education. I. Title.
LC2781.5.M94 2002
378.1′2′08996073—dc21 2001043796

British Library Cataloguing in Publication Data is available.

Library of Congress Catalog Card Number: 2001043796
ISBN: 0–89789–793–5

First published in 2002

Bergin & Garvey, 88 Post Road West, Westport, CT 06881
An imprint of Greenwood Publishing Group, Inc.
www.greenwood.com

Printed in the United States of America

The paper used in this book complies with the Permanent Paper Standard issued by the National Information Standards Organization (Z39.48–1984).

10 9 8 7 6 5 4 3 2 1

Contents

Foreword

This book, about the voices of African American/black women in the academy, could not be more timely and appropriate than at the beginning of the twenty-first century. Black women scholars employed in predominantly white colleges and universities are a rather recent phenomenon. The 1970s started the entry of black women into these institutions, but this entry has not resulted in any significant increase. Most of these African American women have been and are still employed in community colleges or non–major research institutions. Irrespective of the type of institution where these women are found, their voices have been rather silent; and even when not silent, they are often not heard. Through the many efforts to dismantle affirmative action, which benefited white women much more than black women, color-blind ideology is on the rise, and it suggests that race need not be considered salient in achieving equal opportunity. Such ideology and perception are more likely to lead to the silencing of African American women's voices now than in the past. There seems to be an assumption that opportunities are equal for everyone and that racism is practically dead. Hence, sources of black disadvantages are perceived as characteristic of blacks themselves. This view may be characterized by what Thomas (2000) refers to as "anything but race perspectives." In other words, contemporary racism is deemphasized and replaced by nonracial explanations.

This makes it even more critical that the voices of African American women be heard regarding their experiences in the academy. This may be one way to inform academic and lay people that racism and sexism are not dead. These voices are overdue; they need to be in the public arena. They may help to dispel the myth that black progress has led to equality.

Moreover, African American/black women in the academy throughout the United States need to be aware that what they, too, are experiencing are not simply personal troubles but public issues, because the experiences of many other women are the same or similar. White women and men should also be informed. This should help them understand that complaints of unequal treatment from their black colleagues are not simply "whining," as many whites seem to believe.

For those black women in the academy who are so isolated from women like themselves, self-victimization may follow when these others are not available to validate some of the racism and sexism that they experience. This is even more likely to happen when your racial counterparts make you feel that you are just too sensitive or too defensive. There are no guarantees that readers or hearers will heed these voices, but making them public may benefit the victims of racism as well as the perpetrators. If these voices serve no other purpose, they will, it is hoped, help to prevent African American women, and other women of color, from playing the "victim" role.

Essie Manuel Rutledge

Preface

When I wrote *Black Women: Do They Cope Better?* (Englewood Cliffs, NJ: Prentice-Hall, Inc., 1980), and revised it in 1991, my primary concern as an academician was that of Black women's self-concept as it relates to family role performance. That work has its own place in the literary world. Working in academia for the past several years has enhanced my penchant for writing about African American women in the academy.

My desire became more intense as I communicated with other African American women faculty and/or administrators who work in traditionally white colleges and universities throughout the nation. While interacting with these women on various professional occasions, it seems as if I am listening to myself in terms of our experiences of *race* and *gender* within our respective academic environments. It is a strange, and sometimes comforting, feeling to talk with persons whom you may and may not be meeting for the first time and find that they share experiences to such a great degree of similarity. I became convinced that to pursue research on African American women within traditionally white colleges and universities was a necessary goal.

While social scientific literature on African American women in academia has been by no means prolific, the interlocking systems of *race* and *gender* are very noteworthy, and must be expressed through "our eyes as the beholders of our experiences." Such experiences are varied, and may not be uniformly shared by all African American women in academia; however, a very well grounded form of institutional patterns clearly exists. Our everyday acts of resistance and subconscious challenges of our experiences in academia are overwhelming. Therefore, it is very fair to assume that a common thread exists in terms of our experiences in academia. This book addresses that common thread.

I am grateful to several persons who contributed to the completion of this book. First and foremost, I express my appreciation to the sixty-two African American women who provided the narratives about their experiences for this book. To those women who found the process to be "a little too painful" to write about, I seriously appreciate your candid response to my query. I am especially grateful to Essie Manuel Rutledge, who wrote the Foreword and shared some of her experiences without reservation. A special thanks to Djanna A. Hill, a very young soon-to-be Ph.D. who wrote the Epilogue. Her ongoing research with others of her generation will help to continue the conversation.

To my biological sisters, Rosa Wright Thompson and Hattie L. Wright, who are also in academe, I must say thanks for having always been there for me as my support systems in this pursuit.

I must give special recognition to Summer Yates, a very dear student, for her invaluable assistance in the complete processing of the first draft. My initial editor, Susan Oppenheim, deserves special thanks for her patience, and scholarly editorial comments that guided the transformation of an unmarked manuscript into a finished book. I extend special thanks to Keiko Takusagawa, my graduate assistant and Cheryl Cotterill and Carolyn Spurlock for their assistance in production of the final draft of the manuscript. A special thanks to Lori Ewen, my Production Editor, for her support in the final production of my manuscript. To all others who are too numerous to mention in this manuscript—for your constant encouragement, I am grateful.

1

Introduction

A few years ago, I served as an invited distinguished scholar in residence for a week at a very elite all-female college in the Midwest. My responsibilities included delivering a keynote address in a public forum as well as three classroom lectures focusing on gender and multiculturalism in academia. I welcomed the opportunity!

The experience was emotionally rewarding, until I gave my final classroom lecture on women in the workforce, in which I related my experiences as an African American woman in the academy. Twenty minutes after the start of my lecture, the female professor interrupted and asked, "Are you saying that you have experienced more racism than sexism in your academic career?" Then she abruptly concluded, "That's not what you are to talk about."

With as much civility as I could possibly maintain, I politely replied, "I am coming to an explanation of that in my next statements." I completed my lecture and entertained the students' interesting and thought-provoking questions, none of which suggested I should make a distinction between racism and sexism. The events of that classroom lecture engendered a two-page letter from a white male professor who had accompanied me to the classroom and remained to hear my lecture. His letter questioned his colleague's rationale for unethically interrupting my presentation, and copies were sent to high-level administrators. The following evening at a preplanned reception in my honor, the female professor tearfully apologized to me for her behavior in the classroom, saying, "I had some problem with your emphasizing racism more than sexism to the girls . . . and I'm sorry for what I said to you, because I really don't know your experiences." I accepted her apology and enjoyed the rest of the reception.

It is interesting to note that neither the content of the course nor my lecture carried the intention of assigning effectual weight to racism or sexism. Instead, it was about gender, multiculturalism, and my experiences. That situation replayed itself in my mind with heightened clarity as I considered possible motivations for the professor's comments. It is a good example of how white women, who have not been victims of racism, lack a full understanding of the impact racism has on women of color. The events of that classroom lecture led me to question the necessity of choosing, in an effort to raise societal consciousness, which—racism or sexism—holds greater significance in the lives and careers of African American women. Clearly, both "-isms" and all other forms of -isms are an injustice to human beings. People are products of their experiences; determining the repercussions of -isms should be an assessment process unique to individuals.

The classroom lecture experience also illustrates the idea that people have little difficulty assessing their own victimization within the American society's systems of oppression—be it racism, sexism, ageism, heterosexism, or any other -ism. However, at the same time, people typically fail to comprehend ways in which their thoughts and actions can ultimately reinforce and uphold another's subordination.

After my experience as an invited distinguished scholar in residence, I was presented with an important decision. In this book, I could attempt to systematically divide the effects of racism and sexism; however, I felt that in doing so I would compromise my perception of my experiences as an African American woman. The final decision, then, was not a difficult one. . . .

Introduction

I grew up in Mississippi and as a 16–year-old accelerated student began my freshman year at a historically black private college during the height of the civil rights movement. I had a real sense of my experiences of racism—experiences by which anyone undoubtedly would have been affected. Growing up in a time before the feminist movement had fully developed, my circumstances of birth let me know what racism was about. Racism secured far more influence and visibility in my world during that time.

Throughout my academic and professional career, I have learned what it means to be an African American woman in the academy, and I also know that racism still remains alive, well, and dominant. This book makes an attempt to show the impact of racism as well as the intersection between racism and sexism that African American women experience in traditionally white colleges and universities across the nation. It provides qualitative cases of our experiences as faculty and administrators in these academic environments. It is quite fair to assume that a common thread exists in terms of our experiences in academia. This book addresses that common thread based on our experiences.

2

The Status of African American Women in Traditionally White Academia

African American women live in a society that devalues both their sex and their race. The liabilities of the intersection of female sex and black race for these women (which creates a distinct gender) are also evident in the types of occupational roles to which they have been restricted:

> They have been stereotyped as nurturing, scheming, lewd, and unintelligent. In ways parallel to many of the obstacles black men face, they are assigned personally limiting occupational roles—servant laborer, mammy, prostitute, church lady, matriarch, etc. Black women who become professionals, entrepreneurs, or even successful entertainers are often viewed as "strong" black women or else are perceived to be emotionally cold, selfish, and aggressive in unwomanly ways. Missing from the traditional occupational roles for black women, to this day, is a wide-scale recognition of their intellectual competence. (Zack, 1998, p. 81)

Until recently, African American women were excluded from professional positions in traditionally white institutions of higher learning. Prior to World War II, African American faculty and administrators were deliberately excluded by law or tradition from predominantly white universities (Benjamin, 1991, p. 123). However, even with present-day opportunities for greater inclusion, many African American women have found life inside the academy to be fraught with numerous contradictions and dilemmas. This experience is very succinctly described by one scholar as follows:

> It is difficult to talk about being Black in a White space, even though in the United States such is usually the case. The difficulty is to speak, to name, without appearing to whine, a near impossibility, since African American women are not expected to speak at all. It is particularly difficult to be heard since despite reality, the myth still prevails that African American women are making great professional strides. Enmeshed within this myth is the belief that even when African American women are suffering, obstacles are faced stoically and handled with a prayer, and a smile. In other words we always overcome. We African American women are reluctant to dispel this myth for it is one of the positive stereotypes afforded us. (Farmer and James, 1993, p. 205)

The words of Carthy (1992) complement the preceding:

> Black women have been more than victims; they have been actors, conscious builders of relations from which they benefit, and though confined certainly to very limited sphere of the white patriarchal world, their position affords them clear understanding of their oppression. (pp. 43–44)

In one simple statement, Atwater (1995a) has concisely defined a theme present in much of the literature about African American women and the academy: "The very few African American female faculty members currently in academe express feelings of loneliness and isolation" (p. 239). Such a significant theme it is—feelings of loneliness and isolation—that quite often the literature makes it the foundation for a steady assessment of barriers faced by minority women faculty at colleges and universities across the nation. In one study, African American women noted lower satisfaction with professional lives, differential and negative treatment from colleagues, and greater feelings of isolation on campus. Such isolation carries with it important implications: Literature shows that the rate of promotion and tenure among African American women is slower than that of African American men and white women. Isolation and lack of effective mentoring processes are direct influences in these low promotion and tenure rates as well as low retention rates among African American women in academia (Williams-Green and Singh, 1995).

The following literature review is divided into four major sections, each of which addresses the perceptions and opinions of African American women working in academia. The first section will discuss the search process and why recruitment efforts fall short of the ideal, failing to increase the number of African American women faculty and contributing to a continuing feeling of isolation for those women who are presently in academia. The second section will focus on what is often a transitory time for many African American women faculty, highlighting the struggles of finding appropriate mentors, attaining tenure or promotion, as well as the reasons why a strong recruitment plan can quickly degenerate without proper retention strategies. The third section will build upon the information presented in the second section as an overview of ways individual faculty or departments and entire universities can increase the retention rate for African American female faculty. The fourth section addresses coping with challenges in the academic environment.

THE SEARCH PROCESS AND RECRUITMENT

> "Nationally, 2.2 percent of faculty in higher education are African American females." (Atwater, 1995a, p. 237)

This alarmingly low percentage of 2.2 percent (Atwater, 1995a) can be attributed to, among other things, a decrease in the available pool of qualified job candidates (Womble, 1995). However, the potentially largest force in determining the number of African American female faculty is that of the recruitment process, a process that fails to attain positive results because it can be biased.

A reluctance to define critical issues and admit that racism or sexism exists may hinder a search committee's efforts in maintaining true objectivity as they determine the best qualified. With the admission that racist or sexist attitudes can and do exist, committees may be more likely to determine negative effects and correct them rather than ignoring the problem and refusing to allow any change in the process (Atwater, 1995a; Womble, 1995).

How do racism and sexism infiltrate the search process? Much of the literature offers a response to this question, with varied examples. Atwater (1995a) points to the issue of power that enables certain groups within a department or university to create and maintain rules that work in their favor. The increasing number of African American students in higher education is dependent on the presence of African American faculty (e.g., Blackwell, 1989; Epps, 1989). However, even as universities publically embrace a diverse student population, they continue to "employ promotion and tenure guidelines historically detrimental to African American female faculty "(Staples, 1984, p. 5). Groups and individuals with a firm hold on power have the potential to determine the fate of an African American female applicant specifically or any other person generally.

Often it is not the individual or microlevel issues, but larger-scale institutional "structures and cultural climates that prohibit the full participation of Blacks" (Lindsay, 1994, p. 432). For example, to be considered for a high-level position in academe, such as a dean or university president, an applicant must have had previous experience in a similar job setting. African American female faculty who have not had opportunities to gain previous experience (because of racism, sexism, or any of the other numerous inhibitors of success) find themselves in a cycle that can seem hopelessly difficult to end.

Legally, academe is assumed to be strictly prohibited from discriminating in the work environment, but behind closed doors, racism exists in ways that prevent equitable consideration of job applicants.

Lindsay (1997) provides several examples of biases that work against African American women. One example is that search committees often rely on informal social networks to recommend and present possible job candidates—networks that typically exclude minorities—and therefore applicants are not given equal weight in the selection process.

A second example is based on the definition of two types of bias that occur in the selection of employees: statistical bias and informational bias. Statistical bias happens when employers rely on negative group images rather than a direct assessment of the individual applicant. General stereotypes are wrongly accepted as an accurate representation of an individual, and "thus, even for highly qualified minority candidates, exclusion becomes the reality" (Lindsay, 1994, p. 432). The second type of bias, informational bias, happens when an employer values the recommendations of white references more than those of African American referees.

From my perspective, I contend that minority high-achieving professionals are seen as an exception. At the same time, the mediocre past performance of a minority person is attributed to permanent variables (such as inability, personality, or inadequate background), whereas white male counterparts are relieved of lasting negativity brought on by poor past performance with excuses of temporary conditions (health problem, family problems, economic problems, etc.). In many cases, it is argued here, a minority woman is overlooked because students or fellow faculty feel uncomfortable with an African American female in a position of power because she will have the ability to make life-affecting decisions.

MAKING TRANSITIONS

> "Success in academia depend[s] not only on what you know, but also who you know for support, guidance, and advocacy." (Christiansen et al., 1989, p. 58)

Once an African American woman has accepted a job in academe, she will inevitably face obstacles that other faculty are able to avoid.

Gender and race inequities can ultimately hinder opportunities to collaborate with colleagues. It is critical that African American female faculty and universities alike work to overcome the misleading notion that the establishment of mentoring relationships is an unnecessary endeavor. Mentors need not be a minority or female; however, regardless of a mentor's race, ethnicity, or gender, it is important that she or he be aware of the politics of difference (Womble, 1995, p. 250).

Feelings of isolation are greatest when African American women are unable to access valuable networking opportunities. Without positive collegial relationships, minority female faculty may be excluded from the "information loop," therefore missing out on properties held by the "in group" (Womble, 1995, p. 245). Examples of such properties include travel funds, grant money, support services, etc. Research shows that nontenured women faculty and faculty of color were virtually without mentoring, except for mentoring relationships they pursued with each other; this gives credence to the increasing amount of frustration and alienation experienced by African American women who find themselves searching for support with depth and validation (Sorcinelli and Billings, 1992).

The barriers that African American female faculty can potentially face often stem from the fact that minority women faculty constantly have to overcome racial and gender bias to become key players in the informal networks where real decisions are made (Lindsay, 1994, p. 436). Some African American women find that their ideas at times are viewed as legitimate only when white colleagues restate them as their own. Others hesitate in voicing their concerns so as not to be labeled domineering, owing in part to the fact that studies show that women who speak during more than one-third of a meeting's time are perceived as overbearing (North, 1991). Often, the single African American woman faculty member in a department or those hired through programs such as affirmative action are subjected to magnified expectations and extreme evaluations. In certain cases, African American women feel pressure to outperform other (white) colleagues just to maintain perceived equal performance status with them (Phelps, 1995, p. 260)—only to have such outstanding performances discounted as a result of racism or sexism.

All of the above issues that African American women faculty face are clear examples of the "double jeopardy" black women endure in overcoming both racist and sexist attitudes (Brown, 1998, p. 170). A study by McGuire and Reskin (1994) further reinforced the validity of the double-jeopardy concept: The study confirmed that white males had higher levels of authority and salary and that employers discounted the credentials of black women. In fact, the study concluded that if black women were to receive comparable reward, their earnings would increase by $7,000 annually.

In regard to the increasingly male-centered presentation of African American studies, Collison (1999) cites comments from Duke University professor Paula Giddings:

> The new generation of scholars is coming up [at a time] when they don't have to prove the importance of Black women's studies. The best scholars know that you can't look at any history without looking at gender. Black women are at the intersection of race, gender, and class. (p. 16)

Harvard University law professor Lani Guinier acknowledges double jeopardy in the academy, saying, "For too long, Black women have been submerged in the claims of race or in the claims of women" (Collison, 1999, p. 16).

Interaction with other faculty is a key factor in career longevity and success, but it is important to note that the self-worth of African American females cannot be entirely dependent on white faculty. Self-worth and self-reliance must be internally generated; support networks must be established in and out of the university setting (Atwater, 1995a, p. 240).

Mentoring and support networks play a vital role in the career success of African American women in academe. Racist and sexist barriers can be lessened through a combination of interaction and personal determination. Networking with others and adhering to a personal coping philosophy help African American women faculty deal with long-term and day-to-day job pressures (Sorcinelli and Billings, 1992).

RETENTION AND LONG-TERM CAREER SUCCESS

> "Retention requires the profession to listen to the ideas and voices of those African Americans currently teaching, with respect to necessary reforms and strategies." (King, 1992, p. 6)

Although women comprise 27.3 percent of all faculty in American higher-education institutions, research has indicated that African American women represent only 2.2 percent of full-time faculty at institutions of higher education (Gregory, 1999). Furthermore, many of the African American women who do teach are often found in historically black colleges and universities. At predominately white research institutions, approximately 4.7 percent of the faculty in higher education are African Americans, and only 2.2 percent are African American women.

African American women hold only 6 percent of the full professorships compared with 1.6 percent for African American men, 9.9 percent for white women, and 88.2 percent for white men (Carter, Pearson, and Shavlik, 1988). Most African Americans are typically found among non–tenure track lecturers, instructors, and assistant professors, and they also earn less than their white colleagues at those institutions (Gregory, 1999; Fields, 1996; Holland, 1989).

Success in academia is determined largely by the ability to obtain tenure, something that becomes yet another hurdle in the journey for African American women faculty. In fact, it has been said that "if the road to tenure is rough for all women, it is particularly bumpy for women of color" (Phillip, 1993, p. 42). Because many African American women are the only, or one of few, minority women faculty in a department or university, they often feel an obligation to represent the minority—a demanding time commitment for one or two faculty members. Although a minority woman may serve on minority-related committees or advise a department on multicultural issues, these duties are in most cases not given equal value to other contributions in tenure review.

African American women faculty are interested in many minority-related activities (recruiting and retaining African American students, representing multicultural issues at department meetings, etc.) and quite often engage in such projects voluntarily. However, such activities require significant time and effort, taking away from research time necessary for tenure preparation (Phelps, 1995). The extra burden of such service is a detriment to the scholarship of black women academicians; the expectation that they will take the role of a counselor to black students or a "spokesperson" for diversity-related issues limits time ordinarily devoted to research and publication. This limitation in turn, works to silence the dual black/female perspective (Collison, 1999). The overwhelming pressures of service and scholarship are coupled with the stresses of maintaining personal and family lives. Black women are typically more involved in activities such as teaching, advising, and committee service than are some of their white counterparts. Because of these responsibilities, black women may not have adequate time—as white male colleagues have—to conduct research and publish articles (Moses, 1989).

Many minority women faculty members choose to research topics that explore multicultural issues—topics generally published in journals dedicated to such a focus—and in some cases, these journals are not considered prestigious, therefore further limiting tenure possibilities (Womble, 1995). Many students represent minority concerns that research is trivialized and depreciated if it focuses on issues pertaining to Blacks (Exum, 1983).

Research suggests that universities and departments take a holistic approach to their evaluation criteria and that tenure committees redress the present imbalance in the assessed values of teaching, research, and service (Lagowski, 1992; Corbett, 1992). In interviews conducted by Lindsay (1994), one African American woman noted that every single minority within her college had dealt with challenges that were not experienced by white colleagues throughout the tenure and promotion process. African American women at white schools perceive that they will have to work harder for promotion in comparison with their white colleagues; worse yet, these white colleagues often receive their promotions at the expense of the African American women in the department (Edwards and Camblin, 1998).

How rare is tenure among African American women faculty? Consider, for example, the numbers given by Arlene Holpp Scala (1994), who is a women's studies professor at William Paterson College in New Jersey. Of the 216 total tenured faculty at the college in 1994, only 5 were black women.

When a department has only one African American female faculty member, not only does she experience feelings of isolation, but she may also be overwhelmed by responsibilities automatically given to her. The token African American woman may experience situations in which she is painfully aware of her singular status (Edwards and Camblin, 1998). While it can be considered a benefit to be upheld as the department's symbol of diversity and being sought as a consultant on multicultural issues, this role may also limit time that could be used to focus on promotion or tenure. As a result of the large time commitment, faculty often experience burnout and exhaustion. Sole departmental African American woman faculty members cited, as another benefit, increased cross-disciplinary exposure to the university community because of their race and gender; in contrast, however, they felt that often they were appointed to such representation only on the basis of race and gender (Phelps, 1995).

Departments with more than one African American female faculty member provide minority women an alliance of emotional and moral support while at the same time opening up possibilities for research, teaching, and service collaborations. A department with more than one minority woman faculty member serves as a reminder that diversity exists within the African American community. To the contrary, often departments with more than one African American woman faculty member are less accepting of minorities, perceiving alliances that form for moral and professional support as racial alliances that are intimidating or threatening to those in power. One African American woman expressed that in such departments, minority women were compared against each other—comparisons generally made among every faculty member—but a magnified comparison, more salient for African American women because they were compared against only each other, whereas other faculty were compared against the entire department. In such cases, when departmental support is lacking, African American females are able to generate positive work experiences individually.

In a study on black women in academia, more men reported having participated in an orientation program when they took a new position at their institution. African American women reported that they felt less accepted by the white community as a result of not having participated in an orientation program (Williams-Green and Singh, 1995).

COPING WITH CHALLENGES IN THE ACADEMIC ENVIRONMENT

Mentoring other African American colleagues is a critical component of professional and emotional stability. Malveaux (1999) writes:

> Too often, we see younger sister scholars as competitors, not collaborators and inheritors of the dream. Alternatively, some of us are too busy to mentor and are too heavily weighed down by our own pursuits. (p. 22, 23)

African American women faculty can enhance long-term career goals by employing a number of empowerment strategies. Examples of these strategies include understanding that self-validation will sometimes be the only source of acknowledgment, prioritizing time and activities, learning to say "no" without feeling guilty, maintaining mental and physical health, focusing on life outside academia, and finally recognizing that departments often operate according to norms rather than rules (Phelps, 1995).

Various internal motivations become coping strategies for surviving the injustices in academia. African American women frequently push forward in an effort to improve conditions for other African American women and see themselves as "mechanisms for social and institutional change" (Edwards and Camblin, 1998, p. 33).

African American women in academia must find ways of adapting and coping with departmental relations. Different women handle situations in contextual ways; however, there are some consistent coping mechanisms used by African American women faculty. The perceptions of many African American women in academia are reality based. Racism and sexism are accepted as challenges rather than as obstacles or limitations. Many African American women find that acknowledging the reality of racism and sexism is an initial step in developing positive attitudes toward overcoming barriers to success. Family support, spirituality, and community involvement provide the encouragement and reinforcement needed for professional stamina (Edwards and Camblin, 1998).

Bower (1996) writes that prescriptions for successful inclusion of women and minorities all involve commitment and action by institutional leadership. African American women recognize what colleagues can do to support their work, and institutional leaders can show commitment to the advancement of African American women in many ways. Possibilities include highlighting the excellent work of individual African American women faculty, placing the participation and success of minority women high on the list of issues critical to the institution, recruiting qualified African American women for significant positions within the administration, and recognizing and respecting ways in which African American women exercise social and organizational power. Other faculty should be educated about the needs of African American faculty and be committed to making noticeable change. It is not enough to simply tolerate diversity. Instead, it should be accepted and embraced (Phelps, 1995). In the journey toward tenure or other promotions as well as long-term job satisfaction, it is most important that African American women maintain self-confidence because this will help transform predominately white research institutions (Atwater, 1995b, p. 285).

Another study provides insight into the historical life experiences of African American women (Slevin and Wingrove, 1998). The study consisted of fifty African American women who had retired from professional careers either as professional educators or other traditionally female occupations. The authors emphasized the nature of race and gender obstacles and how the women overcame them. This research documents how decades of racial and gender bias—expressed in few options, limited salaries, and blocked opportunities to succeed—shaped the nature of their retirement. The women, ages fifty-three to eighty-eight, were educated during the Jim Crow era. The study provides insight into how race and gender composition suggest a continuous struggle for social justice.

A significant element necessary for contributing to the success of African American women in academia is mentoring. Studies conducted by African American scholars such as Blackwell (1989), Brown (1998), and Wilson (1993) have continuously cited the lack of mentoring as a primary reason why traditionally white institutions have difficulty recruiting and retaining African American and other non-Asian minority students. For example, Blackwell (1983) suggests that the number of African American faculty at colleges and universities is a strong indicator of the first-year African American student enrollment and retention rate and the total number of African American student graduates. Also, many African American students view the absence of African American faculty as paralleling the students' current low status and future outlook on campus (Smith and Zorn, 1981). In other words, the mere presence of African American faculty in college and university settings enhances the image that the students, too, can complete their education and become competent and successful professionals (Defour and Hirsch, 1990).

African American women often experience isolation because of the lack of a critical mass. Many have reported that they need other African American women within and outside the department to share common ideas and concerns. There is also the profound need to affirm each other's presence when the institution fails to do so. Such feelings of isolation and loneliness serve as primary factors for influencing the decision either to remain at an institution or to seek alternative employment (Gregory, 1999; Phelps, 1995).

Numerous African American female faculty have reported that their qualifications are continuously challenged in academic settings (Wilson, 1993; Howard-Vital, 1989). One author affirms this report in her comments:

> Each of us as black women, women of color or white women intimately knows the presumption of incompetence that impacts our careers. We know the negative stereotypes about our ability to reason, think and analyze. (Smith, 2000, p. 31)

Smith goes on to discuss survival strategies for African American women in the academy. Introducing one's credentials from the very beginning and even videotaping classes as a record of excellence in teaching are examples. Another important strategy is for black women to continue to write about their experiences with racism and sexism. In doing this and assessing similarities in experiences across the country, African American women are better prepared to demand both the institutional and the individual support necessary for changing racist and sexist practices (Smith, 2000).

3

Epoch of the Time

As an African American female sociologist, I am not overwhelmed by the notion of naming a specific theoretical orientation for this book. However, critical theory is applicable. A primary characteristic of social theory is that it is a systematic approach to understanding and describing day-to-day life experiences. The focus of this work is to offer insight into the experiences of African American women in academia.

I refer to this chapter as an "epoch of the time" because it is designed to explore a time marked by our assessment of points of reference that ultimately led to historical and memorable events. These events capture a significant role in the lives of African American women.

Today's significant role stereotyping and gender imbalance in the workforce reduce women to subordinate roles—there is no denying such an obvious fact. However, within academic settings, gender inequality is constantly addressed, and it is significant that such analysis is more commonly made by white female scholars than by African American women or their white male colleagues. In fact, contemporary studies of middle-class African American women are rare.

However, studies of those who have persisting experiences of discrimination, despite their educational and occupational achievements, provide strong evidence of the central play of discrimination in the lives of contemporary African Americans (St. Jean and Feagin, 1998, p. 5). One scholar succinctly directed attention to this issue as follows:

> In the contemporary post modern culture, gender is given a very considerable salience; social class and race are not thought to be equally important as determinants of inequality. Where individuality, perceptions of self-worth, and patterns of interaction are weighed so heavily, the social stratification based on racial distinctions and race-based animosities figures less prominently. (Wilkinson, 1998, p. 169)

Judith Rollins (1985) has shown in her research on African American women employees that class and racial experience are typically far more overwhelming sources of oppression than gender experiences. Similarly, Wilkinson (1998) concludes that if race continues to be ignored as a central element in defining the nation's opportunity structure, there will be no understanding of why the American race-based democracy is so often confronted by the "dilemma" that Myrdal (1994) insightfully portrays.

Within the last few years, I have heard many individuals who are naturally insulated from racial discrimination use a widely known phrase to express misguided beliefs that African Americans are "just playing the race card." Interestingly, I have never known anyone to play the gender, ethnic, class, or other "card" in an effort to rationalize inequities in American society. The assumption of "playing the race card" is a convenient escape from accepting and understanding the continuous existence of racism in America. In most instances, the "race card" is already on the table and need not be "played" by the victims of racism.

Granted, few people are familiar with our experiences as African American women in academia. Yet an appreciation of our experiences is critical for grasping the complications and sometimes overwhelming factors that force us to persevere.

Conventional wisdom tells us that we live in a society that is grounded in racism, sexism, and numerous other "-isms." Our ideal participation in a patriarchal, capitalist society is based primarily on our circumstances of birth—circumstances that no person is able to control. The African American and female circumstance of birth is referred to by Essed (1991, pp. 30–32) as "gendered racism," an experience that may be described as a level of "double consciousness" (credited to Du Bois, 1967, p. 5). Within the double consciousness lies a struggle to prove that we are capable of job performances equal to those of white colleagues, particularly white men. This form of gendered racism is seriously embedded in the core culture of the social structure of American society.

Derogatory expressions about African American women in academia remain important dimensions of racial oppression. Discrimination comes in many forms, sometimes subtle, other times blatant. In either case, because the workplace becomes such a central part of one's life, discrimination holds the dangerous potential to weigh down its victims. Some attempt to suppress it, while others readily respond to it; but each victim of discrimination must subconsciously fight the barriers they inevitably face. They continuously look for meaning in the dilemmas of everyday racism.

In many instances, white employers and colleagues believe African American women to be incompetent:

> These workers face stereotyping, excessive demands, an absence of mentoring, exclusion from work cliques, and being ignored and harassed. Frequently defined as workplace "twofers," black women may carry the stigma of affirmative actions hiring, whether they are hired under those circumstances or not. (Yanick and Feagin, 1998, p. 41)

The perception that African American women are incompetent pervades much of their career, forcing upon them the undeserved stress of providing a defense they should not need to give and fighting to prove merit when merit is unquestionably apparent. A typical example of this follows, highlighting the struggles of an African American female full professor being evaluated in the routine budget and merit process:

> In the chair's final write-up for budget and merit, he referred to the African American female professor as "not very competent in teaching," justified by scores in student evaluations that only he [the chair] wrote. "A lot of students have complained to me about the way courses were taught, and they didn't like the grades you gave them," was his comment. Oh, and by the way, one of the two courses taught was race relations and the other was a service course.

In response to her negative teaching score, the professor says, "He [the chair] was not afforded the opportunity to make any negative comments about the remaining criteria (service, research, and scholarship) because my record—locally, nationally, and otherwise—speaks for itself." She further notes that often competence in the three tenure criteria areas is relative, depending on who is judging and who is being judged at a given time, concluding:

> A fair assessment of my judge (white male) is that he is highly intimidated by me in terms of my level of competence in research and scholarship, so the only weapon he could possibly use was teaching. In terms of research and scholarship, I often wonder how it is measured in my department. For example, one white male claims numerous publications mostly co-edited with many others and appearing in generic journals—and he is a full professor. Another white male recently made full professor with only two publications. The committee's justification for his promotion was that he deserved it because he had worked in the department for a long time and was committed. I wonder what he was committed to . . . not publishing for twelve years?

The message is simple. In the continual effort to escape stereotypes and labels of incompetence, an African American female faculty member has to outperform her other (white) colleagues just to maintain equal performance status with them (Phelps, 1995, p. 235).

The force of white male dominance prevails in traditionally white research institutions, affecting women in the academic environment. However, the consequences of such dominance are more intense for African American women and women of color than for other women. Why? Simply because African American women and other women of color are perceived as "outsiders within" (Collins, 1986). Being an outsider within affords them the characteristic of assessing race, gender, and class simultaneously. They can attest to verbal, nonverbal, visual, and nonvisual expressions of oppression. When African American women exhibit any level of assertiveness, they are frequently labeled as "loose canons" who are dealing too much in triviality, playing the race card. Misconceptions and stereotypes about race and sex lead to the treatment of and interaction with African American women as labels, thus mystifying the real persons behind the stigma and encouraging self-fulfilling prophecies by the sex and race that hold power (Kawewe, 1997, p. 263).

What about the Equal Employment Opportunity Programs guidelines as they relate to African American women in academia? Before affirmative action programs, advertising for academic positions was done through the "old boys network," which both intentionally and unwittingly barred women and minorities from access to academic employment. After affirmative action policy was instituted, academic advertisements appeared not only in mainstream sources but also in journals, newsletters, and other media sources targeted toward women and minorities.

Commonalties in employment announcements may seem politically correct: "ABC University is an equal opportunity, affirmative action, equal access employer and especially encourages applications from minorities, women, and persons with disabilities." But what some people fail to realize is the actual practice of recruiting, hiring, and retaining faculty through tenure can be, and often is, manipulated and disguised by both visible and invisible internal forces. It is difficult for others, and sometimes even the employee, to understand exactly what this practice entails. Hence, numerous African Americans in general, and African American women specifically, become victims of this process.

In this chapter, I have identified some of the pitfalls we are subjected to during the "epoch of the time." In summary, African American women in white academe are

1. Subjected to maximized expectations and extreme evaluations in performing our responsibilities.
2. Expected to outperform other white colleagues just to maintain equal status with them, only to have such outstanding performance discounted as a result of racism and sexism.
3. Assumed to be doing "trivial" research if it focuses on issues pertaining to African Americans.
4. Overwhelmed by responsibilities automatically given to us based on our race and gender.
5. Challenged to overcome both racial and gender bias to become key players in the informal networks where real decisions are made.

This chapter has focused on general historical events influencing the lives of African American women in traditionally white educational institutions throughout the nation. The following chapter, "The Power-Thirsty People Syndrome," addresses the affecting forces that contribute to our experiences.

4

The Power-Thirsty People Syndrome

Racism, sexism, and numerous other "-isms" are systems of advantage that provide those of the "right" race and sex with the opportunities and rewards that are unobtainable to other individuals and groups in society. Sometimes they work in isolation from each other, but most of the time they operate in combination to create a system of advantages and disadvantages that enhance the life chances of those of the "right" race and sex while limiting the life chances of those who are not.

What do I mean by the "right" race and sex in American society? I mean that being white, male, and European (or any combination of these) are attributes that suggest privilege and power; consequently, everyone else is perceived as different and less deserving of being treated equally. In the words of Rothenberg (2001):

> Racism and sexism are systems of advantage based on race and sex. In the United States racism perpetuates an interlocking system of institutions, attitudes, privileges, and rewards that work to the benefit of white people just as sexism works to the advantage of men. (p. 96)

The system of privilege in the workplace discussed by Wildman (1996) relates to the experience of African American women in traditionally white academia. She notes that the privileging that takes place in the workplace does not end with maleness; it includes whiteness, heterosexuality, and middle-class values within, American culture. She gives a perfect example of how people in their powerful groups follow unwritten rules to maintain their privilege and power:

> When law faculty talk about hiring, certain criteria and phrases are an accepted part of the discourse, which ostensibly is about the qualifications of the applicant. No one wants to hire an applicant who is not qualified. And so participants in the discourse tacitly agree that the conversation is about evaluating qualifications and eliminating the unqualified. . . . But the conversation that is really going on is not at all about qualifications. The discussants are asking, "Will this person fit into our group, fit into our institution? Will this person change it in any way that will make me not fit, or hurt my place in the institution in any way? If someone comes who is not like me, will I still be valued at this place or have other opportunities?" (Wildman, 1996, pp. 108–9)

The preceding is a typical example of what I call "bookends" of feeling intimidated by women in general and African Americans specifically. This brings to mind a response from one of the African American women in my research who was actively recruited as full professor with tenure at a research one university on the West Coast. As the first African American women hired in that department, she states:

> At the beginning of my first year here, a white male professor demanded that the chair raise his salary equitable to mine because "he . . . had been at this university for more than sixteen years" prior to my having been offered my position. He ranted and raged with the chair until the chair asked him to put in writing his justification for an increase in his salary comparable to mine.

> Oh! By the way, he had been employed at the university for sixteen years, had only five publications in some "generic" journals, and was made full professor one year prior to my going there. I wondered why he had not tried to negotiate a salary equitable to what the other few full professors in his department were making once he got promoted. Of course, the dean did not honor his request.

I have some knowledge of the African American woman's track record in the case cited above. She had numerous funded research grants, at least twenty-three articles published in leading journals in her discipline, and five books—three of which were singly authored and the remaining two co-authored with one other woman. This is a prime example of a white male's perception of power and privilege over women in general and African American women specifically. It appears that the thought of hiring an African American woman full professor with a salary higher than his was emotionally devastating to him—because he was white and male, and had been free all his life. Hence, he tried to utilize the power and privilege seemingly accorded to him based on his white maleness. His behavior certainly parallels racist and sexist ideology. It also suggests that his concern was not about qualifications, because her qualifications far exceeded his. His concern was about the questions that Wildman (1996) raised: "Will this person fit into our group, fit into our institution? Will this person change it in any way that will make me not fit, or hurt my place in the institution in any way? If someone comes who is not like me, will I still be valued at this place or have other opportunities?" (pp. 108–9).

Numerous whites, Europeans, and men (or any combination of these) capitalize on the attributes of power and privilege at the expense of others who do not possess those attributes. They appear to be bound to promoting a hostile work environment for women in general and women of color specifically.

Male dominance creates power differences between men and women. It also promotes the idea that men are superior to women. We live in a society that is patriarchal to the degree that it is male dominated, male identified, and male centered. At the very core of this patriarchal society is the oppression of women.

One of the most fundamental questions raised by the women's movement is not a question about women at all, but rather a question about men: Why do men oppress women? (Pleck, 1993). Two kinds of answers are given to this question:

> The first is that men want power over women because it is in their rational self-interest to do so, to have the concrete benefits and privileges that power over women provides them. Having power, it is rational to want to keep it. The second kind of answer is that men want to have power over women because of deep-lying psychological needs in male personality. These two view are not mutually exclusive, and there is certainly evidence for both. (Pleck, 1993, p. 221)

Pleck (1993) suggests that in order to account for men's need for power over women, "it is ultimately more useful to examine some other ways that men feel women have power over them than fear of maternal domination" (p. 221). He identifies two forms of power that men perceive women as holding over them, which are directly related to traditional definitions of adult male and female roles and which complement a feminist perspective. The first form of power that men perceive women as having over them is expressive power, the power to express emotions. Implicit in this form of power is that traditionally in male/female relationships, women are expected to express their needs for achievements only imaginatively through the achievements of men. Pleck states, "It is not so widely recognized, however, that this dependency of women on men's achievement has a converse" (1993, p. 222). Although this form of expressive power may have an element of truth in the personality of men, as indicated by the author, it raises a very important question in my mind: If maleness means power and privileges, why must the oppressors (men) depend on the oppressed (women) to express their emotions for them? If maleness provides the power and privilege embedded in the concept of maleness, then, the power and privileges should develop and enhance their ability to express their emotions. It seems to come easily in dominating and oppressing women, so why not in expressing their emotion?

The second form of power that men attribute to women is called masculinity-validating power. This is described as the way in which men experience themselves as masculine based on the role women are expected to perform in making them "feel masculine." Pleck notes further that clearly in the encounter with women, men are not so much seeking sexual gratification as validating themselves as men—which only women can do for them. If women refuse to exhibit their expressive power in validating their (men's) masculine-validating power, many men feel lost and bereaved or rather lacking in whatever they perceive themselves to be. Hence, they may attempt to frantically force women back into their accustomed and/or traditional roles historically prescribed by society based on their gender. Pleck concludes that

> men's dependence on women's power to express men's emotions and to validate men's masculinity has placed heavy burdens on women. These are powers that men have themselves handed over to women, by defining the male role as being emotionally cool and inexpressive, and as being validated by heterosexual success. (1993, p. 222)

Power, like love, is a concept used both implicitly and explicitly, simultaneously, in day-to-day behavior by some individuals. It is understood by some of us but rarely defined by others. An individual's assumed power transcends privilege and becomes a desire to control and create systems of race and gender inequity. This abuse of power serves as a deterrent to social mobility for all women. Yet it eats at the core of what some white males perceive to be the epitome of "keeping African American women in academia in their place."

Some white male colleagues frequently discuss and publish concerns about issues of gender inequities, battered women, alternative lifestyles, and promoting racial and ethnic diversity—and oppress African American women at the same time. This type of behavior is clearly contradictory to the issues they claim to support. The devastating fear of losing power over others motivates some of them to act in racist and sexist ways.

It has been confirmed that institutional structures exist to serve the needs of individuals and groups who control inordinate power, authority, and resources within the social system and who simultaneously limit the access of others to the advantage of power (Blackwell, 1991). This is particularly related to the occupational structure of traditionally white colleges and universities throughout the nation. Despite the earlier notion of affirmative action policy, the entry of African American women faculty in educational institutions remains deliberately slow. Why? Simply because the academic occupational structure continues to establish and maintain parameters in an effort to deter academic mobility; this is the case for women in general in academia and more specifically for African American women. It is difficult for an African American woman to enter traditional departments of the academic setting and even harder for them to move past nontenured positions that are associated with minority programs (Benjamin, 1991).

The powerful are reluctant to practice inclusive measures that threaten to diminish their status and privilege. Typically, those with power are under no pressure to create standards of equity in the department because they are the unquestionable majority. The majority of tenured professors are white males, aged thirty-five to fifty-five, with unlimited time in their given positions. Untenured faculty is composed largely of women and minorities, an obvious detriment to collaborative work that seeks to cut across diversity (Greenberg, 1995).

The power to determine tenure—or, in essence, to decide another's future—rests comfortably in the clenched fists of white male faculty everywhere. It should be noted that white men are not the sole abusers of power; so are some white women. However, in many instances, the firmly established status of white men as the advantaged group makes their role in the system difficult to challenge successfully.

Why are white males so fiercely protective of power? The underlying reasons go deeper than just a desire for personal success. In the rules of the operating academic unit exists a traditional understanding that personal success comes in the form of another's failure. African American women are consistently working to stand their ground personally and professionally; part of this struggle originates in the attempts of the powerful to maintain a comfort level, or equilibrium, at all costs. Their role has been accepted for so long that any opposition is likely to be met with defensive measures and alienating practices.

Dividing power is a dangerous move because with the elimination of the inner circle of privilege comes an abrupt shift in the system; change is by no means welcomed. According to Morgan (1986), "People and departments often cling to outdated job descriptions and resist change because their power and status within the organization are so closely tied with the old order" (p. 172). Oftentimes members of the privileged group will establish standards for untenured faculty but, more importantly, minority faculty that they themselves cannot meet. The rationalization often given by those who determine another's future is that "this is a new day" or "the bar has been raised." This type of nonsense is a clear way to ensure that minority faculty members are always excluded.

When the comfort level of the powerful is threatened, they revert to exclusionary or alienating practices aimed at restoring balance and protection to their position among the ranks. Over time, some faculty members become supportive of the elite power group and see conformity to the set standard as the only measure of success. As one author writes, "Eventually, virtually all members of the organization become, for all practical purposes, predominately occupied with the task of protecting their backs rather than working to achieve the avowed goals of the organization" (Harvey, 1989, p. 274) and consequently succumb to the wishes of the powerful. They try to write like them, publish in journals acceptable to them, and present papers at professional meetings they define as acceptable. In other words, the minority faculty has accepted the chase without recognizing the game.

The priority becomes securing one's place in the mainstream and joining networks of colleagues that are categorized by levels of power. The powerful instinctively cling to one another and develop a mutual understanding that they must join forces if they wish to be a vital part of the system. Without a mentor or an alternative ticket into the group, the African American woman is automatically denied access to informal networking that determines the outcome of departmental decision making. These alliances between faculty are difficult to break because power is carefully handled so as not to fall into the hands of an outsider. If the chain of control is broken, the legitimacy of power is overturned. Members of the power network guard their status in subtle and strategic ways, always working to keep others down. The work of minority faculty and especially African American women faculty is criticized on grounds such as "It is co-authored" or "It is the wrong journal" or "It is qualitative and not quantitative enough." African American faculty and, to some extent, all faculty of color are, like the race dog, always "chasing the rabbit."

Rewards are bestowed upon the independent achiever, providing the people in power no incentive to work cooperatively. The motivations of monetary gain, prestige, tenure, and recognition—among other rewards considered to define success—are focused on individual rather than collective efforts. For those who are insecure with themselves personally or professionally, the importance of power to validate self-image is all consuming. Powerful persons will do anything to prevent power from being stripped away, because without it, judgment and evaluation from colleagues are based on individual merit alone. The power serves to mask their weaknesses; hiding safely behind this facade, the powerful magnify the trivial faults of others as a diversion to their own shortcomings. The fear of the inevitable loss of power appears to be emotionally destructive to certain white male colleagues.

Power can be formally defined as the medium through which conflicts of interest are ultimately resolved. Power influences who gets what, when, and how (Morgan, 1986, p. 173). Morgan (1986) quotes political scientist Robert Dahl, who defines power as "an ability to get another person to do something that he or she would not otherwise have done" (p. 174). It is important to understand not only the dynamics of power in higher education but also the historical basis for the establishment of such power. In other words, how did certain people come to power? Morgan (1986) writes:

> Many organizational conflicts often become institutionalized in the attitudes, stereotypes, values, beliefs, rituals and other aspects of organizational culture. In this socialized form, the underlying conflicts can be extremely difficult to identify and to break down. (p. 170)

Those who inherit control and privilege over time do so through the employment of key tactics. The powerful are those who have control over scarce resources—not necessarily full control, but enough to pull strings in a timely and effective manner. Power involves not only control over information that is released but also control of information that is not released. Giving people privy to certain information ultimately determines who will become a member of the circle of power.

White women, of course, are often able to become members of the circle of power. As Franklin and Richardson (1972) write:

> Because the power relationships between blacks and whites and between men and women in this society have been imbalanced, there is a complex pattern of power relationships between the four gender and race groups—white males, white females, black males, and black females. (p. 239)

White men have historically enjoyed the greatest power and prestige. The values, ideology, and policies of the superordinate group control primarily the distribution of power among subordinate groups. Being white in the eyes of the dominant group is assumed to be superior to being black. Consequently, white women have enjoyed greater power than either African American men or African American women.

Critical structural changes can be the subtlest of tactics to minimize the influence of others and maximize control of key figures within a department. Control of important information and technology can significantly alter relations among faculty. By defining the boundaries of an organization, many come to power by either isolating the department as an independent unit or by pushing it to interact with outsiders. To keep the department operating within its designated boundaries, members often "control admissions through selective recruitment" (Franklin and Richardson, p. 182).

Selective recruitment is evident in many higher-education settings in which African American women enter. As one writer states, "Even when Blacks are invited for interviews, they are frequently treated insensitively, which discourages them from accepting a position" (Benjamin, 1991, p. 125). For the African American woman who makes it past the initial efforts to eliminate her presence, an entirely new set of behaviors surface as faculty members sense their power slipping. To keep their status, the powerful exercise controls that keep others from escaping the rank into which they have fallen. In one study, more men than women indicated that they had participated in a welcome or initiation program after accepting a new position (Williams-Green and Singh, 1995). This practice keeps the social group intact without admitting unwanted members who are not trusted to conform. The same study indicates that the African American women sampled expressed lower satisfaction with institutional efforts to recruit blacks. As a result of such practices, African American women reported that they felt less accepted in their academic communities and were much less satisfied in the level of interaction with the white majority community.

Social controls, as discussed by sociologist Peter Berger (1973), are used by those in power to manipulate others: for money, to be accepted and appreciated, and so on. Those in power are able to alter and recreate the prevalent expectations of the department, thus significantly affecting the opportunities for others to be included or excluded. According to Berger, an adherence to the informal code of conduct set forth in a group setting is "just as essential for one's career in the occupation as technical competence or training" (1973, p. 76). African American women possess the technical competence and training; however, when they are denied access to the inside network that determines and enforces the informal code, they are prevented from reaching their greatest potential. The time and energy spent fighting to gain access to important information within the department are barriers to African American women who are balancing numerous responsibilities. Yet, without this needed information, these African

American women are unable to participate in the critical decision making that takes place within the network of power.

Faculty who are the originators of the informal codes that exist in higher-education settings know that the only way to make such codes seem valid is by protecting them from the scrutiny of outsiders. Berger (1973) writes of institutions that individuals also create "procedures through which human conduct is patterned, compelled to go, in grooves deemed desirable by society. And this trick is performed by making these grooves appear to the individual as the only possible ones" (p. 87). A cycle begins, in which faculty members use their power to control others; in turn, as others realize their career is on the line, they respond. As they respond to the controls that are handed down, the power begins to accumulate and controls become stricter.

The self-appointed informal leaders of a department may take on a variety of roles in their interaction with others. Depending on context, people may act in one way in the company of their allies and differently when attempting to control others. For example, a white male faculty member might take the role of the protector or mentor, expecting that the African American woman might then feel obligated to support his decisions or his alliances with and against others. Some may take the role of the intimidator, others of the hero, and so forth; however, regardless of the role, when that role is threatened, the individual will act to reclaim his or her position immediately. If the power role is validated, then he or she will attempt to continue that role in order to evoke the expected response from others. As Berger (1973) says, "Even very intelligent people, when faced with doubt about their roles in society, will involve themselves even more in the doubted activity rather than withdraw into reflection" (p. 97).

Thomas and Znaniecki (1927) have written that if people define situations as real, they become real in their consequences. Those faculty members who possess the power in a department become the forces that define situations. By keeping a tight control over information and resources, the powerful can determine what others know or do not know. Along with the power to define situations comes the ability to influence the silence of others. If the powerful can win over everyone in a department, the sole outsider may be hesitant to question the reality that is so easily accepted by others. This is a means of keeping a hold on power—through pressure to conform and alienation of those who diverge. The powerful arrange relationships among colleagues who are certain to succumb to this pressure and consistently remain loyal to their interests.

The preceding discussion provides an explanation of power and privileges that is grounded in racist and sexist ideology. It clarifies the reality of race and gender in American society. As put very succinctly by Brittan and Maynard (1984):

> It is our contention that the way in which gender and "race" are socially constructed (in Western society at least) is dependent to a large degree on the practice of domination. The practice of domination in our sphere is never insulated from its practice in another sphere. Those who exploit workers do not have difficulty in exploiting black groups. Those who dominate their wives and children at home have no difficulty in dominating people at work. What we are saying here is that oppression is indivisible. Where there is oppression of women, we find oppression of out-groups; where we find economic oppression, we discover sexism and racism. (p. 180)

Those of us who refuse to succumb to this pressure become the victims of its wrath. Therefore, it is fair to assume that the experiences of African American women in white academe are qualitatively different from those of white women within the same settings. This chapter, "The Power-Thirsty People Syndrome," has addressed the inequalities of power as they are related to racism and sexism in institutions of higher education. Its primary focus has been on how African American women in traditionally white colleges and universities are affected by the force of power that is often grounded in paternalism. The chapter that follows provides insight into this concern with a discussion of "Interpretive Views of Race and Gender."

5

Interpretive Views of Race and Gender

It is fair to ask the question: What is the nature of racism and sexism in society today? While attention to the intersection of racism and sexism in the experiences of women of color is very recent and very limited, it is evident that patterns of disadvantage for African American women are both different and often more severe. The existing literature has shown that African American women are twice as likely to experience racist and sexist acts of harassment as white women (Ries and Stone, 1992; Benokraitis and Feagin, 1986). The stereotypical perceptions of African American women have been used to blame them for the overall social and economic disadvantage of being African American in a white patriarchal society (e.g., Billingsley, 1992; Collins, 1989; Myers, 1998). We African American women have been perceived as assertive, aggressive black matriarch's who intimidate or dominate men and are nonconformists to roles appropriate to the female gender, among other negative views.

Hooks (1981) sets an interesting tone in describing the intersection of race and gender for African American women in America when she writes:

> No other group in America has so had their identity socialized out of existence as have black women. We are rarely recognized as a group separate and distinct from black men, or as a present part of the larger group "women" in this culture. . . . When black people are talked about, the focus tends to be on black men; and when women are talked about, the focus tends to be on white women. (p. 7)

In 1989, Hooks emphasized the fact that we as African American women must resist oppression by identifying ourselves as subjects, by defining our own reality, by explicitly naming our history, and by telling our own stories in what is known as "self-definition" (p. 43). According to Johnson-Bailey (1994):

> In order to understand how racism practices are evident and propagated in the professionalization of adult education, we must remember that what happens in higher education settings to a great extent mirrors what is happening in the culture at large. American society is, after all, one of hierarchies, and it is therefore inherently one of divisiveness and power struggles. To be an African American in this country is to be relegated by birth to a position of implicit inferiority. (p. 66)

The author states further that race is clearly a major problem in American society, as is gender. However, the two are rarely seen as co-conspirators. They do combine in a real sense in the lives of African American women.

Many individuals have found it difficult to accept and respect differences in human beings as ordained by a generous Mother Nature. As one writer so poignantly states:

> As result of the masculine morality, something of great significance happened to the male in pursuit of manhood and superiority through violence, psychological as well as physical. He failed to develop a healthy capacity to love and to relate to people as human beings and not as objects to his exploitation. In his

> moral and emotional inferiority, he often scorns or hates instead of loves in his insensitivity to other people, especially if they were women or ethnic minorities. Among the emotional and moral cripples, who find pleasure in doing evil, are millions of racists and sexists. (Braxton, 1973, p. 21)

According to Marable (2001), racism and sexism combine with class exploitation to produce a three-pronged mode of oppression for women of color. He discusses the fact that in terms of economics, African American women and other women of color rank far below white women when it comes to income, job security, and employment mobility. Emphasizing that racism and sexism are not perpetuated biologically, like a disease or drug addiction, Marable suggests that both behaviors are learned within a social framework and have no ground in hereditary biology (2001, p. 127). The reality is that both racism and sexism are grounded in stereotypical beliefs, and myths about African American women abound in the academic environment.

There is a reservoir of resentment and bitterness in many white Americans, particularly white men, regarding any effort to eliminate discrimination by giving preferential treatment to people of color, who are seen by these whites as undeserving or as having already benefited enough from programs for enhancing equity (Stein, 1998, p. 88).

As a point of debate over race versus sex, it may be argued that one has an order of significance over the other. In the words of one scholar:

> But clearly, race and sex are more than just symbolic phenomena. They are the hard facts of social reality. To be a member of a particular race or sex brings with it different opportunities, rights, and constraints. The study of semiotic systems must therefore be complemented by an examination of such material constraints, or how they operate and shape our life experiences. (Guillaumin, 1995, p. 1)

Curry (1995) describes her dialogue with a white female philosopher on oppression, racism, and sexism at a regional philosophy conference prior to publishing her work "Racism and Sexism: Twenty-First Century Challenges for Feminists." Curry observes that the white female philosopher's definition of oppression was very much like "Arthur Britain and Mary Maynard's definition found in *Sexism, Racism, and, Oppression*: as those who are . . . coerced by others. . . . Their freedom of action is limited by the superior power of those who are in a position to insure their compliance" (Curry, 1995, p. 19). Curry interprets the philosopher's definition of racism and sexism to equate with that of Lorde in her *Sister Outsider*, where she defines racism as "the belief in the inherent superiority of race over all others, and thereby the right to dominance," with the definition of sexism as "the belief in the inherent superiority of one sex over the other, and thereby the right to dominance" (Lorde, 1984, p. 115). She states further that "the same woman rejected the claim that African American women are more oppressed than white women and that racial oppression is greater than sexual oppression" (Curry, 1995, p. 19). However, Curry tells of how another white female philosopher conferee expressed opposition to the first white female philosopher's position. Both of them, as well as others, were quite vocal in pointing out personal experiences and in giving arguments in support of one or the other of these too frequently asserted positions (Curry, 1995, pp. 20–21). Curry states, "I thought to myself that we could continue this mode of discussion at length and still not resolve the issue" (p. 20). She suggests that as an African American female philosopher, she, too, could have shared extremely bitter and hostile, but subtle, experiences of racism and sexism and "formulate other arrangements" in support of each of the white female philosophers. In this part of Curry's writing, she raises some very important questions as to the similarities and differences between black and white women's perceptions about which one of the two—racism or sexism—is more important or, rather, has the most effect on both groups of women. Her conclusive comments for their part of her discussion are as follows:

> For many African American women, most white women deny racism as well as important differences between African American women and white women that are manifested by racism and sexism. For many white women, most African American women deny the significance of sexism as compared to racism. (Curry, 1995, p. 20)

Curry provides several typical examples of African American and white women's standpoints about racism and sexism in an effort to show how we may become able to resolve "their impasse by confronting our differing standpoints and widening our perspectives on oppression" (1995, p. 20).

African American women are a discrete group with dual statuses as blacks and women. Historically, they have encountered a myriad of barriers since their forced arrival to America. Throughout the twenty-first century, obstacles to upward mobility and equal life chances have confronted them. No other racial or ethnic group in the United States has been as enslaved or faced such perpetual racial segregation and discrimination in all institutional domains (Wilkinson, 2000, p. 115).

In examining the empirical (historical) analysis of the impact of race over gender, Wilkinson (1991) addresses the paucity of data that exist on the nation's work history where race, class, and sex intersect in occupational and income disparities. She states:

> With respect to this, it has been noted that contemporary sociological examinations of women in the labor force have tended to accentuate two strata: (1) poor women or those in the bottom ranks of the stratification hierarchy, typically low-income minority welfare clients, or (2) academic and professional women. (Wilkinson, 1991, pp. 87–88)

Upon review of Wilkinson's social historical analysis of the segmented labor market and the plight of African American women from 1890 to 1960, it should not be difficult to imagine the resounding effects of racism as the dominant force in their lives. Complemented by the writings of Brewer (1988, p. 339) and Blauner (1972, p. 23), Wilkinson concludes:

> The persistent influence of race in the social and economic order confirms earlier job discrimination and wage disparities under industrial capitalism, . . . and that slavery established unearned privileges and preferential treatment for white males and females and that these were "expressed more strategically in the labor market and the structure of occupations. . . . If there is any one key to the systematic privilege that undergirds a racial capitalist society, it is the special advantage of the white population in the labor market." (1991, p. 99)

Wilkinson advises the reader that "further research should also be guided by realistic and objective paradigms which take into account sustained disparities in occupational achievements and career mobility by gender and race as these articulate the past" (1991, p. 99). The concern here is that

> when studies of occupational and income inequality are made, serious consideration should be given to the historical record of slavery which perpetuated unceasing discrimination and entrenched racial stereotyping of African American women. The influence of the past legacy of slavery should not be ignored "if we are to gain a clear understanding of the present occupational, income, educational, and privilege dissonance between African American and White women even when education is controlled." (Wilkinson, 1991, p. 99)

One might readily ask the question: What is all this "busy talk" about race and racism? Numerous people wish to think that racism is a thing of the past. One case in point is provided by Tatum (2001). She discusses how early in her teaching career, a white student whom she knew inquired as to what she would be teaching the following semester. She told the student she would be teaching a course in racism. In a very surprised voice, the student asked, "Oh, is there still racism?"

(p. 100). Having assured the student that racism still exists and suggested that the student take the course, Tatum states:

> Fifteen years later, after exhaustive media coverage of events such as the Rodney King beating, the Charles Stuart and Susan Smith cases, the O. J. Simpson trial that appeal to racial prejudices in electoral politics, and the bitter debates about affirmative action and welfare reform, it seems hard to imagine that anyone would still be unaware of racism in our society. But, in fact, in almost every audience I address, there is someone who hasn't noticed the stereotypical image of people of color in the media, who hasn't observed the housing discrimination in the community, who hasn't read the newspaper articles about documented racial patterns at the local school, who hasn't seen the reports of rising incidents of rising hate crimes in America–in short, someone who hasn't been paying attention to the issues of race. But if you are paying attention, the legacy of racism is not hard to see, and we are all affected by it. (2001, p. 100)

It is fair to assume that the words cited above are not directed at the student's naive inquiry into the existence of racism, but that some white people resist acknowledging that racism is alive and functional in American society. Consequently, as Tatum's work shows, many white people prefer to define racism in terms of racial prejudice because by adopting this definition it is possible to say that African Americans as well as white people can be racist. In the words of Rothenberg (2001):

> For many people in this society, being able to say so seems to satisfy a deep emotional need. Confronted with behavior or speech that is hateful, they wish to use the strongest words they can to condemn and deplore it. Once racism is defined as a system of advantages based on race, it is no longer possible to attribute racism to people of color because clearly they do not systematically benefit from racism, only white people do. This, of course, does not deny that people of all colors are capable of hateful and

> hurtful behavior, nor does it prevent us from taking them to task for their prejudice. But it does mean that we will reserve the term "racism" to refer specifically to the comprehensive system of advantages that work to the benefit of white people in the United States. (p. 96)

There are different views among blacks and whites in our society as to how and where racism creates a source of conflict and stress for those of us who are affected by it. One scholar suggests that

> for many white Americans, the word "racism" is a red flag. They don't see themselves as harboring animosity toward black people as such; they believe they hold to an ideal of equality, and of equal opportunity. So they feel insulted to be called racists, baffled by charges that we live in a racist society. A white supremacist would not be so wounded. . . . In general, white people today use the word "racism" to refer to the explicit conscious belief in racial superiority (typically white over black, but also sometimes black over white). For the most part, black people mean something different by racism: They mean a set of practices and institutions that result in the oppression of black people. Racism, on this view, is not a matter of what's in people's heads, but of what happens in the world. (Lichtenberg, 1998, p. 43)

The fact is that racist attributes do exist within the oppressors and are exhibited in unequal treatment of African American women in traditionally white colleges and universities throughout the nation. As Lichtenberg (1998) states further:

> Racism as overt or out-and-out racism reflects a powerful strain in our attitudes toward moral responsibility. . . . On this view, you are responsible only for what you intend; thus, if consciously you harbor no ill will toward people of another race or background, you are in that respect innocent. For those who would be deemed the oppressors, such a view is abetted by what psychologists call "cognitive dissonance"—essentially the desire

> to reduce psychological discomfort. It is comfortable for white people to believe racism is dead just as long as they harbor no conscious feelings of antipathy or superiority to blacks. And conversely, it is less painful for blacks, seeing what they see, to think otherwise. (p. 44)

I agree wholeheartedly with Lichtenberg's interpretation of how whites perceive their racist behavior toward others who are different. I also contend that it is not our responsibility as African American women in traditionally white academe to interpret why the systems of oppression exist and function against us in our daily lives. Oppressors have to live with their own consciousness or what psychologists call "cognitive dissonance." It is not our responsibility to try to reduce the psychological discomfort for those affected by it. However, we as African American women in a white, male-dominated society are very capable of recognizing the oppression, while challenging those practices by whatever means necessary.

Refusing to recognize differences in race and gender experiences of African American women and other women of color makes it impossible to see the problems of oppression facing all of us as women. Thus, in a patriarchal power system where white skin privilege is a major prop, the entrapments used to neutralize black women and white women are not the same (Lorde, 1998):

> Black women and white women are not the same. For example, it is easy for black women to be used by the power structure against black men, not because they are men, but because they are black. Therefore, for black women, it is necessary at all times to separate the needs of the oppressor from our own legitimate conflicts within our communities. This same problem does not exist for white women. Black women and men have shared racist oppression and still share it, although in different ways. Out of that shared oppression we have developed joint defenses and joint vulnerabilities to each other that are not duplicated in the white community, with the exception of the relationship between Jewish women and Jewish men. (p. 536)

On the other hand, some white women are lured into joining the oppressor under the pretense of sharing power. This possibility does not exist in the same way for African American women. The tokenism that may be sometimes extended to African American women is not an invitation to join power; our racial "otherness" is a visible reality that makes that quite clear. For white women, there is a wider range of pretended choices and rewards for identifying with patriarchal power and its tools (Lorde, 1998, p. 536).

As I write about Lorde's comparison of African American and white women's experiences, I reflect on an interesting experience that lends credence to her analysis. While attending a national conference recently, I was conversing with three colleagues (white women in academia). One of the women, who had previously been a full professor at a research one university, told us that she had been offered a tenured full professor position at what she called "a little rinky-dinky university with no research reputation" by a white male chair. The white male chair had negotiated a "package deal" of $15,000 more than what she was making at the institution where she had been employed and a teaching load of one course per semester in order for her to do research. She accepted the position. But she was in for a rude awakening: She told us that before the end of the first academic year, she observed that the white male chair had created serious conflict among colleagues, based on his sexist, racist, and heterosexist views. She stated, "I walked into an academic environment controlled by a white male whose negative views about those who were different were the order of the day, and no one else knew anything about everything other than he." I asked her, "Did you get an assessment of his behavior from other faculty members, or was it based on your own observations?" Her response was, "Nobody had to tell me what kind of person he was. . . . It was clear in frequent conversations with him, when he made verbal assaults, expressions of sexual harassment, and defamation of character of colleagues, while suggesting that I [not] associate with them." Another one of the women asked her why didn't she align herself with other colleagues. Her answer was based on the fear that "he would not take care of [her] as he had promised." The bottom line is that the woman became a team player in the small camp of the very few people who thought like the white man and whom he could control and manipulate. This is where small-group dynamics come into play, which prohibited her from aligning herself with those who were not a part of that small group. Therefore, she had become a part of the "mix" based on what both she and the white male perceived as power.

Some scholars agree that the "intersectionality" of black women's lives is not recognized in much of existing literature on race and gender. We are said to be discriminated against in the same way as black men or white women. Therefore, there is little recognition that we are discriminated against as both (Scales-Trent, 1989; Krenshaw, 1989; Smith, 1991). Despite, or perhaps because of, the dual factors of being African American and female with their negative effects on life opportunities for us, our problems often go unrecognized.

Let us begin here with the interpretation of Scales-Trent (1989). She prefaces her article with the following: "I woke up this morning, I could see and I could breathe. . . . Are there any rights I'm entitled to?" (p. 9). According to this scholar:

> The economic, political, and social situation of black women in America is bad, and has been bad for a long time. Historically, they have borne both the disabilities of blacks and the disabilities which inhere in their status as women. These two statuses have often combined in ways which are not only additive, but synergistic—that is, they create a condition for black women which is more terrible than the sum of their two constituent parts. (Scales-Trent, 1989, p. 9)

Smith (1991) discusses the interaction between racial and gender oppression relative to the legal ramifications for African American women:

> Creating a critical consciousness that recognizes the distinctiveness of Black women's expressions has been an ongoing concern of Black women who have a "shared awareness of how their sexual identity combines with their racial identity to make their whole life

> situation and the forms of their political struggle unique." From a range of perspectives, they have posed a common question: How does the law account for the unique social and historical location of Black women whose realities often encompass the interaction between racial and gender oppression?" (p. 21)

Drawing on the Civil Rights Act of 1964 (Title VII), the most comprehensive federal status covering employment discrimination, Smith views Title VII as "having been of limited use for Black women, due in part, to the law's categorical approach to equality: racial ethnic groups in one category and women in another" (1991, p. 22). This results in the fact that courts tend to be most responsive to black women's claims based on three circumstances where race and sex are identified as distinct and isolated concepts. These circumstances are (1) racism only, (2) sexism only, and (3) racism and sexism separately—the last of which Smith calls "interactive discrimination" or disproportionate and adverse specificity. Although Smith states that she does not believe that there is a monolithic black women's reality from which it follows that every black woman necessarily constructs her identity to embrace a fusion between race and sex, she does contend that "the employment experiences of many Black women manifest the interaction between racism and sexism" (1991, p. 23).

Frequently, the importance of race is obscured by white Americans. As Grillo and Wildman (1996) put it:

> Like cancer, racism/white supremacy is a societal illness. To people of color, who are the victims of racism/white supremacy, race is a filter through which they see the world. Whites do not look at the world through this filter of racial awareness, even though they also constitute a race. This privilege to ignore their race gives whites a societal advantage distinct from any advantage received from the existence of discriminating racism. (p. 87)

The authors suggest further that many white people think that African Americans are obsessed with race and find it hard to understand the emotional and intellectual energy that they devote to the subject (p. 98).

St. Jean and Feagin (1998) conducted research on subtle gendered racism experienced by African American women. The data were secured primarily from interviews with 101 women from a national data set of 209 interviews with middle-class African Americans. The sample consisted of a median age of just under forty years and median income of $47,000. Approximately 90 percent of the women had a college degree or graduate degrees or had attended graduate school. The researchers also drew on comments from a focus group that included one African American male in a national sample and on comments by a white male and two African American female participants with racially intermarried couples in Nevada (p. 181). The focus group respondents had at least one year of college and a median family income of $50,000. For the analysis, the researchers examined interviews for the use of the term "subtle" as it related to discrimination and for incidents where racial and gender meanings were blurred or less obvious. From a large pool of incidents, they used statements from seventeen respondents whose demographic characteristics matched those of the broader sample. Some of the responses were about the general nature of discriminatory practices, whereas others recounted specific instances of discrimination. Occasionally, references were made to sexual harassment. However, the women's primary concern was not with particular expressions of gendered racism, but racism in general that originated from whites, including white women (p. 181). Therefore, the researchers often referred to white society, or to whites, instead of a white male society.

In presenting the results of the women's experiences of subtle racism, St. Jean and Feagin focused on racialized discrimination that the women faced in everyday life. They noted that even though some blatant "door-slamming and exclusionary" forms of racial discrimination have all but disappeared from U.S. society, many forms of overt and covert discrimination have persisted and subtle and sophisticated forms have developed. An example of this was expressed by one of the female respondents as follows:

> I think discrimination still exists. I just think it's a different way that it's shown. It's more subtle. I guess. I always see myself, though, always having to be a little bit better than my counterparts. So, it's still there, but it's better, it's better. (St. Jean and Feagin, 1998)

The respondents periodically emphasized the point that contemporary racism no longer uses explicit Jim Crow symbols but often promotes exclusion for allegedly nonracial reasons. Such was expressed in the words of another African American:

> Well, you don't see signs, we don't see signs anymore that say "For Whites Only" or "Blacks are not allowed." . . . I guess people find ways in which they can discriminate against you. They find other things in order to keep you out, or "We're looking for a man for this job," or "Do you have these qualifications?" And sometimes those qualifications may or may not be necessary. It's just a way of screening. . . . I think it's like that everywhere. People find ways to screen out what they don't want. (St. Jean and Feagin, 1998, p. 182)

As subtle as it may appear, any form of racist practice is rooted in American history and culture. Even some whites who may be proponents of equal rights can be perpetrators, without necessarily being aware of their behavior in transmitting subtle racial messages. Such was evidenced in the response of another respondent:

> Subtle racism is what I notice among all kinds of [whites], whether it's professional, peers, whatever. Just racial attitudes and assumptions that people make, and usually they aren't aware that they're revealing this to you, obviously. (St. Jean and Feagin, 1998, p. 183)

From their research, the authors concluded:

> In most cases, black women interpret their blended racial-gender experiences with more emphasis on racial factors, thereby maintaining their connection to the situations faced by black men. . . . Less often do they connect their conditions to those of white women. (St. Jean and Feagin, 1998, p. 17)

Johnson-Bailey (1999) conducted a unique qualitative research project relative to race, gender, and class. The sample consisted of re-entry graduate and undergraduate African American women aged thirty-four to fifty-four, of which the researcher was also a participant. It is important to note that the researcher, who was also a re-entry African American woman, was interested in examining the narratives of the women in an effort to determine how the dynamics of the larger society, which often negatively impact their lives, were played out in higher education (p. 659). Using the subtitle "Between Us Women: Bridges Called Race and Gender," Johnson-Bailey merges the theoretical perspectives of Du Bois's "double consciousness" and Collins's "outsider within."

The results of Johnson-Bailey's research showed the following:

> All the women in the study possessed an understanding of societal hierarchical forces that shaped and determined their existences. They identified racism as the specific dominating factor and they used an opppositional world view to frame their stories. . . . Gender, while not advanced by the women in this study as a restraint to their lives or educational endeavors, was observed to be the factor that consistently affected their lives. This was most apparent around issues of self-esteem, childcare, household chores, and relationships. During the interview the women in this study communicated gender-bound assumptive connections when they discussed children, husbands, household responsibilities, doubts, and fears. (1999, p. 660)

Johnson-Bailey's position is that the issues of race and gender were uniting forces in her research. She states that throughout, the women and she established an "ease" when discussing race and gender. She concludes that "our concepts of and our experiences with race and gender were similar" and there was no lack of trust expressed by the women regarding her position relative to race and gender issues (1999, p. 660).

Although the issue of race was not raised in the interview schedule for the research described above, each woman of her sample advanced the concern of how she perceived racism in early life. Race and knowledge of living in a race-conscious society were very real to the respondents. Many of the women described their early experiences of being black as feeling inferior compared with others in American society. They shared their accounts of "knowing" about racial differences in a segregated American society. There was an early awareness of race as narrated by all of the women including the author.

Johnson-Bailey's study (1999) has serious and profound relevance for me and for this book. My early awareness of race while growing up in Mississippi, when my experiences of racism preceded my experiences of sexism, no doubt can intertwine with similar feelings experienced by other African American women. The chapter "Our Voices about Our Experiences" follows.

6

Our Voices about Our Experiences

My reflections for this book complement what Powell (1983) so poignantly stated:

> Historically, the Civil Rights and Black Power Movements were transforming for all kinds of people—black, white, male and female. These movements were the political training grounds for thousands who would later be active in anti-war, anti-nuclear, women's and continuing Black community organizing. It was a time of open resistance and defiance, when many of us tested the limits set by our oppression to see how far they would give. (p. 285)

With those movements came several social and political benefits for some oppressed groups. However, oppression remains omnipresent in the lives of many African American women in academia as we approach the twenty-first century. The following discussion is a scenario that is frequently enacted in our everyday lives.

In discussing my experiences in academia, I must first return to descriptions I presented in the introduction to this book. Having grown up in Mississippi, at 16 years old, I began my freshman year at a historically black private college during the height of the civil rights movement. My experiences of racism—experiences by which anyone would have been affected—were very real. My circumstances of birth let me know what racism was about; however, I grew up at a time before the profound period of consciousness raising about sexism had fully evolved. But it was very clear to me during my early years that to be denied the opportunity to drink from a water fountain marked "White Only" was not because I was a woman. The fact that I could not enter any white-owned and/or -operated restaurant and be served food was not based on the fact that I was female. All of my early education was restricted to an all-black school—not because I was female, but because I was black. When I began college, I lived fewer than eight blocks from the one traditionally white four-year coeducational state university in Hattiesburg, Mississippi. I could not attend that college—not because I was female, but because I was black. This all brings me to where I have been in academia for the last several years.

Another experience at a traditionally white institution stands out in my mind: A statement on one of my student evaluations at the end of a term read: "I was told by one of my professors not to expect to learn much in this class—but I learned a lot." I read the comment but did not think much about it until the next term, when a white female student stopped by my office to discuss a project about violence against women during the following term. She asked me, "Did you see the comment that I made on your teaching evaluation?" Knowing that students remain anonymous on evaluations, I asked her, "What was the comment?" With a noticeable level of naiveté, she continued, "Professor X [white male] told me to go ahead and take your class but not to expect to learn very much, but I learned a lot." Was that one for the books! I believed her. I realized that this was a case of a white male perceiving me as lacking in knowledge of social psychology—a specialty in which I am very well prepared. He expressed this to a young white woman, who later told me that I was the first African American teacher she had ever had. The fact remains that such questions are often raised about the expertise and knowledge of African American women, despite the fact that we come from the same universities and academic backgrounds. Some of us were even trained in universities that outrank those from which some white women and men graduated.

A few years later, I chose to teach a graduate seminar, one that I had taught in previous years at the same university. Through some unexplainable decision made during the graduate committee meeting, I was denied the opportunity to teach the course that term. It was instead assigned to an untenured white female assistant professor.

Being aware of the fact that a system of rotating courses among the faculty who had earned Ph.D.'s in that specialty had been proposed earlier, I inquired about why it was decided I could not teach the course. After discussing this with a few colleagues, I got responses ranging from shoulder shrugs to "You know . . . I really don't remember how they came up with that decision."

I have kept written documentation that the same white male professor mentioned earlier, who told the student not to expect to learn anything in my class, also stated, "As long as I am in my present position, Lena Wright Myers will never teach another graduate course." Well, I did teach the course later. This is a prime example of racism that was totally contradictory to this man's facade of staunchly supporting women's rights and racial equality. I can also document comments made by white male colleagues when referring to the work of certain specific African American women, even in the face of traditionally irrefutable excellent records in grantsmanship and publishing, such as: "She is a prolific writer and researcher who is known nationally—but her works are mostly about blacks and are lightweight."

Even though African American women in academia do speak the English language, there is the tendency for some whites to interpret what they think we mean. On numerous occasions, I have served on committees and advisory boards in traditionally white university settings. As I began to make statements about the issue being discussed, invariably someone with personally assumed authority would say, "Professor Myers means that you should think about the issue this way." That person—typically a white male—would continue to explain to the group what he thought I meant, until I would ask him not to speak for me. Clearly, this type of behavior suggests that African

American women in academia need an interpreter and are not capable of saying what we mean. It also indicates a serious need to exude a level of domination or, rather, to exhibit control.

At the same university, in 1995, I was giving a final exam. Students were given their term papers as they turned in their exams. As a white female student received her term paper, she looked at me and shouted, "How can you give me a D+ on this paper?" Before I could explain the reason for the grade, as was already noted on her paper, she walked a few steps away from the desk where I was seated, turned around and threw the paper at me, and again shouted, "You don't like me anyway! I'm going to tell the dean on you, black bitch." She then stormed out of the classroom, kicking over a wastebasket that was at the door, and continued to shout from the hallway, "Fuck you, black bitch!" It took all the emotional guts I had to avoid stooping to her level; at that moment, my main instinct was to take every measure possible to ensure I would never again be called a black bitch by her. After she left, six students remained in the classroom, still taking their exam; all of them gave testimony to her conduct in a judiciary council. She was given disciplinary probation for the duration of her undergraduate education at the university.

My reminiscence of that experience brings to mind another more recent incident—harassment by a young white male student, which shows that African American women can be victims of not only demeaning acts of male dominance but harassment as well. On two consecutive days, as I sat in my office with the door closed and worked with my graduate assistant, a white male student enrolled in one of my classes opened the door, walked directly to me, and, standing less than eighteen inches from me, asked, "Where is my exam paper?" He was referring to exam papers that were returned to the students some time earlier, during his absence from class. When I attempted to go over to a table to get his paper, he moved with me. In other words, each time I moved away from him, he moved toward me. When I said, "Please don't stand so closely as we talk," he replied, "I'm not doing anything." He finally left my office. I closed the door behind him and resumed work with my graduate assistant, who remained in the office during both encounters. Within less than two minutes, there was a loud knock on my door, at which time I asked, "Who is there, please?" Then came the voice, "Me." I opened my door, and there he stood, saying, "You don't like me, do you?" I responded, "I like all of the fifty-eight students in that class—and I don't want to continue a verbal confrontation with you." Again, he left the office, but the next day, much of the same behavior continued, plus he left a threatening message on my office answering machine. Through the assistance of the judiciary council director and the campus police, the problem was finally solved (at least I hope so).

I had another experience in which I was accused of tampering with my student evaluations. At the end of spring term, I had gone home for the summer, as I traditionally do. I received a letter from one of my white male colleagues, encouraging me to hurry and sign my contract for the next year. At the end of the letter was the statement, "By the way, I want you to give me the names of students who delivered your evaluations to the department office last spring." Considering the fact that I had not been asked such a question during my career in academe and since I could not recall the names of the students, I asked other colleagues what this was about and if they had received such a request. They informed me that they had no knowledge about such a request. I had been experiencing health problems during the latter part of that spring quarter, so I decided to concentrate on my health as opposed to worrying about this matter. I was not contacted again about the evaluations, so I assumed it must not have been that important.

However, when the budget and merit committee met later that fall, I received a response to my appeal from the same colleague who had requested the names of students. It read: "I wrote to you last summer asking you for information about problems with your student evaluation forms and did not receive any responses. . . . Our concern about the way you handled student evaluation forms, without any input from you, led this fall to a series of changes that everyone must now follow." (The change was to seal the envelope and both student and professor sign their name across the seal.) When I asked for a one-on-one conversation about the reason for such a request, he nervously stated, "We just want you to give us the names of the students."

After that, my response in writing to him and the committee was as follows: "If the budget and merit committee is basing my teaching evaluations on their assumption that I have mishandled student evaluations in some way, they must be able to back up such an allegation with documentation. Therefore, I am requesting that you and the committee either formally charge me in writing along with documentation to back up such an allegation or drop the matter entirely." I never heard anything more from the colleague or the committee.

Some experiences can be devastating, to say the least. Thus far, I have discussed some of my experiences in academia. Examples of the experiences of other African American women are included in this book. Our lives in academia may result in different expressions of our experiences. The accounts and commentaries of African American women are very important because we have realistic, first-hand knowledge of every aspect of our lives and specifically experiences in academia. Therefore, we are better judges of our experiences than any nonblack outside observer. Let us listen to another African American woman who chose not to remain anonymous: *Essie Manuel Rutledge*—who also wrote the Foreword to this book—shares her experiences as follows:

My experiences in predominantly white colleges and universities are related to administrative and faculty positions. These experiences have been and continue to be varied, complex, positive, negative, satisfying, frustrating, and stressful. Since this book emphasizes racism and sexism, I will lend voice to my relevant experiences.

To recall such experiences is painful, and it conjures up anger because racist and sexist experiences are the result of ascribed statuses over which one has no control. Furthermore, it is frustrating to face the reality that many who enjoy racial and gender privilege are completely insensitive to the fact that their privilege results in benefits that do not accrue to women and men of color, even when meritocracy should be the rule. Those who enjoy white and male privilege take certain things for granted. There are some consequences that they do not have to think about. White men and women do not have to consider race as a factor in how they will be treated, perceived, or judged, nor do white men have to consider their gender in these regards.

Because race is less salient for white men and women and gender is less salient for white men, there is an insensitivity that they carry around that exacerbates the frustration felt by those of us who are victims of both racism and sexism. The frustration is strongly felt when the racially privileged (1) deny that they have privilege and act as if whatever benefits they have accrued are the consequence of merit and (2) dismiss as too defensive the frustration and sometimes anger of those who lack racial and/or gender privilege.

An early experience in my academic career related to racism. This experience involved the merger of a black junior college (at which I was an instructor) with a white junior college in the South. The initial merger resulted in the black college becoming a campus of the white college. After the merger, the administration of the white college and the dean of our (black) campus decided that the faculty should have training workshops conducted by faculty from the main white campus. All faculty from our campus were black, and all faculty who conducted the workshops were white. It was apparent that we, the black faculty, were not perceived as competent to fulfill our responsibilities in a predominantly white college, in spite of the fact that we had been a very successful faculty in the predominantly black college. This was very insulting, to say the least. The black faculty resented it, but no one openly opposed the workshops.

However, I was so insulted by this experience that I questioned the dean on our campus, but in private. She did not seem to feel that there was anything wrong with having white faculty who were our peers teach us what we already knew. Every black instructor had more than nine years of teaching experience, but these workshops concerned what was expected of new faculty.

Unfortunately, our black dean was assigned the onerous task of carrying out the mandate of the white administrators regarding the fate of the black campus faculty, including decisions about who was to be retained and dismissed in the final merger. The decisions were both politically and racially motivated, and they resulted in only tenured black faculty being terminated, while untenured white faculty were retained. This involved eight black faculty members, including myself. This disappointing experience occurred at the height of the civil rights movement, a time when black people had rising expectations that justice and equality would become reality. But because now I was fully aware that those rising expectations were very far from reality, my dreams were shattered.

This experience, which was an outgrowth of desegregation, was only the beginning of a long-standing saga that continues even today. Subsequent experiences are related to my employment in predominantly white colleges and universities in the Midwest. In these places of higher education, I have encountered racism and sexism from department chairs, deans, and colleagues, but in many cases it is difficult to disaggregate the effects of race and gender. However, there are certain markers or indicators that are more discernible for one than the other. When discussing my experiences, I will explain whether I feel race or gender was more salient and why.

My first full-time tenured position after receipt of the Ph.D. (sociology) was as chair of an African American studies department, a position that I held for eight and a half years. I was the only female chair in the college, and there was one black male chair who was African. The racism and sexism were structural, or institutional, and personal. One of the most obvious biases I discovered during my first year of employment was a disparity between my salary and the salaries of other department chairs who were comparable with me in terms of rank, credentials, and years of service. All other chairs, except for one black man, were white males. When I brought the salary disparity to the dean's attention, he investigated it and agreed that salary inequity existed. He then recommended to the provost that I receive a salary adjustment of $150 per month. The provost's response was there was no money for salary adjustments. Hence, I lost $1,800 a year, amounting to a significant loss over the years.

I also remember instances during department chair meetings, held regularly by the dean, when I would make comments or suggestions that were passed over. Yet when the same or a similar comment was made by a male chair, it was given attention. However, the black male chair was treated more as an equal than I was. Gender seemed somewhat more salient than race, but together they had an interactive effect.

In general, there was little university support for the African American studies department. The dean provided money for hiring tenure-track faculty, but otherwise we operated on a bare-bones budget. We had very few funds for programs, equipment, or student employment. The dean left after I had been there for three years. Then, overall, the support for the department began to diminish.

The African American studies department became a "safe place" for black students, where the faculty (a total of three) and chair served as mentors, advisors, and confidants. In addition, the students also called upon us frequently to participate in their activities, but none of this was considered significant in our tenure and promotion decisions. Overall, black faculty were expected to do more than white faculty but received fewer rewards. This is an experience echoed by many black faculty on predominantly white campuses throughout the United States.

Throughout my term as chair, the student enrollment in African American studies classes was mostly black. In spite of my efforts to encourage other departments to advise students to take our courses, it did not happen. There was a widespread assumption on campus that African American studies courses were for blacks only. I particularly tried to encourage education and law enforcement departments to advise their students to take our courses. Students who choose a major leading to careers in these disciplines are highly likely to come in contact with African Americans. Therefore, to me, it seemed apparent that these students would benefit significantly by taking African American studies courses. However, this was not a sentiment shared by other chairs and faculty advisors. It soon became very obvious that the African American studies department and its curriculum occupied a second-class status in the university. It was treated differently than the traditional white departments.

In January 1985, the African American studies department was changed back to program status, at which time I was transferred to the department of the academic discipline in which I was trained. In this department, there was only one black professor, an African man. A whole new saga of racism, sexism, and outright viciousness began then and continued for more than fifteen years, the worst years of my academic career.

This saga began the semester prior to my transfer. This transfer became imminent after African American studies lost its departmental status, because all faculty, according to the university's policy, were required to be affiliated with an academic department. The one other tenured faculty member and I were transferred to the traditional departments of our academic disciplines. The authority to make transfers when a department was eliminated was vested in the president of the university. On the basis of my credentials, the department to which I would be transferred was obvious. However, I do believe that because it was the president who made the decision, and not the department, from the very beginning I became the victim of the latter's wrath.

The first thing that happened after the transfer became official was a request from the department for me to make a presentation about my research/scholarship. The request was delivered verbally by a faculty member who was not in my discipline, which was a subliminal message of rejection by those colleagues in my discipline. Furthermore, I was asked to make the type of presentation that is required of candidates who interview for tenure positions. Please note that at this time I had been employed at the university for eight and a half years and, was a tenured full professor. I had received tenure and promotion to full professor by going through the same process and by meeting the same standards as all the other faculty in my college. Hence, for the department to expect me to give such a presentation was insulting and demeaning. It was a clear signal of institutional racism.

Nonetheless, I agreed to meet with the department faculty, under the condition that we would share with each other our research and scholarship and other common interests. Yet the department's request raised some critical questions in my mind: Why did they expect me to give a presentation? Was this to indicate that they must give tacit consent to my transfer, since they had no authority to approve it? Was this their way of indicating their perceived dominance over me? Be reminded that this was a department composed mostly of white men, one black man who was African, and approximately three white women, but no black women. Furthermore, some of those who had been granted tenure had met much lower standards than were required when I was tenured (the president, who was hired one year before I was, initiated much stiffer standards in the area of research and scholarship than were previously required). Nevertheless, it appeared to me that the department was attempting to exercise white dominance.

Upon physically moving to the department, I was assigned an office that had been a storage room for the college. It was located on a hallway, away from my department's faculty, alongside the faculty of other departments. Moreover, I occupied the office alone. This was fine with me; however, all other faculty members shared offices. Thus, I was marginalized from the very beginning. In other words, I was both physically and socially isolated. Little social interaction took place between the other faculty persons and me. One person with whom I had served on a university committee before joining the department passed by me for about a year without ever speaking. This same person, a white male, had vigorously attacked me in the presence of others, but in my absence.

One of the first acts of racism, after the transfer, was related to my teaching assignment. The chair, along with an associate dean, insisted that I teach African American studies courses. To teach these courses was not a condition of my transfer, but I was told by the chair that I had a "moral obligation" to teach courses in the program. Surely, I objected to anyone deciding my moral obligations. This coercion to teach African American studies courses was continued until I was given a retraining leave to study aging and gerontology. After this, I was assigned to teach courses in the gerontology master's degree program. Once I completed a certificate in aging, I was then released from further responsibility of teaching African American studies courses. No other faculty person in my department, male or female, was ever coerced to teach African American studies courses. However, some of the faculty had specialty areas that were the same as mine. At that time, the program was in dire need of teachers for courses because it had no faculty, but no one volunteered.

Another experience of racism relates to alleged white student complaints. A different chair of my department came to me in person or wrote me about student complaints; some of these were that I did not give back their papers as soon as they wanted to receive them and that I used examples of racism and sexism that they did not like. The chair never gave me names of students or specific examples of their complaints. He always refused to identify the students, even after grades had been given, on the basis of their request for confidentiality. However, the chair seemed to have complete disregard for my due process. Thus, I could not respond objectively to the complaints. Hence, I was placed in a no-win situation that rendered me helpless in either evaluating the complaints or defending myself.

Acts of racism toward me have not been limited to those by department chairs but have included faculty as well. One white female faculty member in the department really demonstrated her racism recently by indicating to one student, who wanted to take a gender roles class from me, that she did not recommend me. When I informed the professor of the student's report, in a letter that I copied to the chair, dean, and provost, she viciously attacked me. However, it should be noted that prior to her vicious attack, she had responded to an e-mail (draft of my official letter) that I inadvertently sent her. This was really a "blessing in disguise" because her responses to the e-mail and the official letter were so different that they are analogous to the characters of Dr. Jekyll and Mr. Hyde.

In the e-mail, she apologized if she had hurt me. Then she commenced to tell me about her respect for my opinions and even stated that over the years she knew I had been mistreated by faculty in the department and that she had often defended me. But in her official letter, she attacked me viciously about what she alleged students had told her about me for more than fifteen years. It was obvious that she was now addressing the administrators to whom she copied the letter. Her attack was slanderous and void of any evidence; indeed, her alleged complaints from students had never been communicated to me over the supposed fifteen years to which she referred. I suggest that any complaints probably had to come from white students because I teach very few students of color. Furthermore, my colleague indicated that most of the complaints were from students in the gender roles course. Is it surprising that to teach about gender by examining race and class might upset students whose traditional, conservative views are challenged? Is it further surprising that a professor who teaches little about women of color would attack one who does? More egregious and racist than the professor's attack based on alleged student complaints was her conclusion that I needed help to improve my teaching and that she would be willing to do a classroom visit and offer suggestions for organization, teaching style, or any other issues that I believed she could help with.

I found this woman's arrogance and racism to be unthinkable and contemptible. She says that she is not racist—but most racists say this. Is she so naive or ill informed that she really does not know what racism is? Her comments are both racist and paternalistic. Does she think that her "whiteness" is a sufficient qualification to judge my pedagogy? She has never visited my classes. Moreover, the fact that I have had many years of successful teaching from the junior high school level to junior and community colleges and to the university exacerbates the extent of her racism. I am not a novice in this profession.

This same woman who feels that she can help me improve my teaching decided to teach a black women's course that I developed while teaching at a previous university and added to the African Studies department's curriculum in 1978. This professor has done no research on black women and had never taught a black women's course. Moreover, she includes little to no information about African American women or other women of color in her gender courses. The material she assigned for the black women's course is a disgrace to the lives of black women; she used a fictional work with a 1940s setting about a black girl who obviously wanted to be white, and it was assigned to be read for the topic of women in slavery. Very little research or scholarship by African American women in the social sciences was included in her course reading material, and what was included was minimally relevant to the course topics that she selected. This colleague was definitely not qualified to teach the course; however, she was approved to teach it, whereas I, who developed it and taught it for more than twenty years, was not asked. I do not believe that I would have been allowed to teach a course for which I was not qualified. This woman, a director of a women's studies program, appears to be trying to control the content of all courses cross-listed in the program, this one included. These actions are unquestionably racist. But the woman in question thinks not—which makes her behavior especially insidious.

Another example of my experience of racism in the setting of higher education was a situation in which an all-black search committee, choosing candidates for an African studies position, selected applicants to call by phone when the dean, a white female, decided that all applications had to be reviewed by the associate dean, a white male, before we could call them. Subsequently, the committee met with the dean to discuss her decision. Members of the committee had taught courses in the department; hence, we were the best qualified to evaluate the candidates to recommend to the department chair. However, the dean refused to change her decision. Therefore, the committee resigned, considering the dean's action to be paternalistic and racist, and unprecedented.

In answer to the question of whether racism or sexism has had the greatest affect on me in academia, I would say that in many instances they are intertwined. In some cases, though, race has been more significant than sex, especially when the perpetrator was a white female; but even then, my experiences show that white females tend to show more respect for black males than for black females, an indication of sexism. When a white male is the perpetrator, both sexism and racism are salient. In my experiences, white males show much more favor toward white females and black males than toward black females. This is even truer when the female is outspoken, independent, and assertive.

My experiences of inequality, involving both white men and while women in the academy, are indicative of racism and sexism. In some cases, racism and sexism have separate effects on African American women, while others interactive effects. But even when they are interactive, to me race is more salient. But for African American/black women, the combined effects of race and gender are greater than the separate effects of either one.

My observations in the department about which I speak were that the white women deferred to men. Consequently, the treatment of these women was reflective of the era of the "cult of true womanhood," when white women were more or less placed on a pedestal, but, as it was then, women of color do not fit the ideal of "true women." Therefore, the privileges granted to white women then and now are not bestowed on African American women. However, that ideal further reduced white women to a subordinate status, but it made them feel far superior to women of color, in spite of the fact that their special status was inferior to men's. Any treatment that signifies inequality is not what I desire, but I do desire equal treatment and social justice.

Furthermore, a major problem is the fact that many white faculty "do not seem to get it." They do not acknowledge or even seem to be aware of the possibility that they engage in the rule of false universalization. They see all women through the lenses of white women. Thus, whatever is perceived as true of white women's experiences is perceived as true of women of color. I am the only African American faculty member in my department, male or female. Therefore, I am often rendered invisible. The faculty seem colorblind, not in terms of seeing and treating me as an equal, but in terms of overlooking my competencies, contributions, and my different experiences. Because I have collegial and professional relationships outside of the department, I have never depended on the department for professional or scholarly validation. Thus, my relationships outside of the department have been a basis for my social agency.

Sociologically, how do we analyze these experiences? We could decide that these are personal problems, but upon further examination we find that they are public issues. Many African American women in the academy have had and continue to have similar experiences. Knowledge of such widespread experiences make us sociologically aware that the structures of inequality, in race and gender, are widespread in society, even in the academy. White privilege is a major prop for racism. Even though it is denied by many, racism is still pervasive, no matter how subtle and covert it might appear. It is still evident that those in decision-making positions (power) tend to serve the interests of their group. My experience fully bears out this assumption, an assumption that is germane to understanding power and conflict relations, and no structures of inequalities demonstrate this perspective better than racism and sexism.

There are very real differences in terms of race, sex, age, class and other characteristics that make people different. But those differences do not separate us. Rather, it is our refusal to recognize those differences and to examine the distortions that result from them and their effects upon human behavior and expectation (Lorde, 1998). Therefore, fair but general definitions of the concepts of racism and sexism for this book are as follows: Racism is the belief in the inherent superiority and dominance of one race over all others and thereby the right to dominance. Sexism is the belief in the inherent superiority and dominance of one sex over the other and thereby the right to dominance.

The preceding discussions by Lena Wright Myers and Essie Manuel Rutledge should provide the reader with subsequent common themes identified by other African American women faculty and administrators in predominantly white institutions. Common themes such as patronizing, disrespect for knowledge, unethical behavior, structural impediments, and numerous other examples are indicative of the impact of racism as well as the intersection between racism and sexism.

THE RESEARCH

The presented data are based on detailed narratives written by sixty-two African American women at traditionally white colleges and universities throughout the country. The sample included African American faculty and administrators from both private and public four-year colleges and universities and community colleges. Respondents were from various disciplines, with the ranks of instructors to full professors. The sample included two recent retirees who "spent almost a lifetime" at the very reputable research one universities from which they retired. The process of data collection was via e-mail and regular mail: Fifty-three responses were received via e-mail and nine responses via postal mail. The instrument used for data collection is as follows:

Lena Wright Myers
Professor of Sociology
Ohio University
Athens, Ohio 45701

(740) 593-1375 (office) or (740) 593–1350 (department)
e-mail: myersle@ohiou.edu

Dear Colleague:

I am in the process of completing a manuscript about African American women in traditionally white colleges and universities (both faculty and administrators in all disciplines). I am reviewing the realities of our experiences primarily from the structural/functionalist and the conflict perspectives, respectively.

Complete anonymity for this manuscript is secured both legally and professionally, unless you suggest differently. Only you will be able to identify your comments qualitatively, once the book is released. Therefore, I have systematically selected you among the numerous distinguished female faculty/administrators in traditionally white colleges and universities in the U.S. for this research pursuit. I welcome your response to your experiences in both past and present positions. Your anonymous responses will be included in a chapter entitled: Our Voices about Our Experiences. Our voices need to be heard! I am asking you to please respond in narrative form to the following general issues where applicable:

1. Early experiences relative to how the persons with whom you work perceive your ability to fulfill your responsibilities as faculty/administrator.
2. Your experiences of racism on the part of your assumed superior, i.e., chairperson, dean, students, etc.
3. Your experiences of sexism on the part of your assumed superior, i.e., chairperson, dean, students, etc.

4. Which of the two practices (racism or sexism) would you say had the greatest effect on you? Please explain why you chose this practice.
5. What is your present rank at the college/university where you are presently employed?

Please respond via e-mail or regular mail to the addresses given above.

It is important to note that pseudonyms are used for the respondents to assure confidentiality.

OUR VOICES ON HOW WE ARE PERCEIVED IN FULFILLING OUR RESPONSIBILITIES

The African American women contacted were asked to please respond in narrative form to the general issues, where applicable, noted in my survey letter.

Ruby, a tenured full professor who had spent the last nine years in a traditionally white research two university in the Northwest, notes her views in responding to the first question of the survey (*early experiences relative to how the persons with whom you work perceive your ability to fulfill your responsibilities as faculty/administrator*):

> The most memorable event regarding my others' perception of my abilities as a faculty member occurred immediately after I received my Ph.D. and my first position as assistant professor in health science and administration. I was told by a white male colleague that while I might be qualified for the position, I would be hired only because I was "black." This was something to which the white faculty alluded on many occasions during the first three years of my tenure at the university.

She goes on:

> I was interviewed for a faculty position by the white male vice president of academic affairs. During the interview, he answered the phone, filed papers, and made at least two phone calls as I re-

> sponded to his inquiries. I finally stopped and stared at him. He then announced that he "liked me because I was a female—and an African American woman with class."

According to Ruby, the question that came to mind was: *Is he proposing to recommend me for the position for which I am interviewing based on my race, gender, and class only?* What about my strong credentials?

We may observe from Ruby's narrative that the white male obviously perceived her to be unqualified for her position. Hence, he substituted her race (black) as the rationale for her having been hired. In addition, other white colleagues frequently substantiated his (white male) claim by indirectly implying the same reason.

In the second part of Ruby's narrative, it seems to be clear that the white male vice president of academic affairs thought very little of her presence as an interviewee, considering the numerous other activities he performed during the interview. In addition, his patronizing remark that he "liked [her] because [she] was a female—and an African American woman with class" implies the same thing: Ruby was not qualified for the position.

Anne, a professor at a university in the Midwest, tells of her earlier experiences as follows:

> In this university and community, I have had experiences that were affirming and uplifting as well as experiences that were demeaning and depressing to the soul and the spirit. I have felt until quite recently that my opinions in my department were not respected in the same manner as opinions of some of my colleagues. I attribute that attitude to a complex interaction of race, rank, and gender. In faculty meetings, I have had colleagues, primarily senior and male, simply talk among themselves when I am making a point. Alternatively, I often hear a talking point or a suggestion for action that I make in a meeting repeated by a colleague, most often male, within five minutes of my contribution. However, the colleague, as well as others around the table, most often accept the point as having been made by whomever has in fact restated my original point. In es-

> sence, my ideas in meetings are quite often not attended to or are appropriated by others during the discussion. This pattern is not entirely unique to me; it is most often the experience of junior women. However, this has not been the experience of the one male African American colleague in my department. Most recently, within the past year, my colleagues have begun to attend more closely to my contributions. This change of heart did not coincide with my success in gaining tenure, an event that occurred four years ago. I attribute this change in heart to my increasing prominence in campus politics, my friendship with the executive vice chancellor (a woman), and the consolidation of my research reputation in the national arena. Until my worth was validated by outsiders (e.g., the chancellor who was an Asian male, the media, federal funding agencies, and national foundations), the white men in my department were less than eager to accord me full inclusion into their "club." This reluctance has not been evident in their relationships with untenured white males nor with the one African American (tenured) male in our department.

In Anne's experiences in white academia, recognition of her opinions came later in her career at the university. She attributes the slow-in-coming recognition to the intersection of race, rank, and gender. It is also interesting how she emphasizes the fact that her statements are often claimed and restated by white male colleagues. This is seen as her not being perceived as intellectually competent, which then requires whites to interpret for her what she means and thus claim her constructive intellectual suggestions as their own.

Carla held an administrative position at a university on the West Coast. She describes her experiences as follows:

> Though my credentials and background far surpassed that of my predecessor, many colleagues assumed there was an obvious administrative error in judgment. Numerous previously disinterested persons asked whether I was the right person for the position. They wanted to know if I would change the character

of the operation. The previous director questioned whether I could be trusted to handle the needs of a diverse community (though I was an active community volunteer with credentials for proof). Shouldn't there be a revision in the checks and balances of the money, and who should be responsible for distribution? Maybe my reporting relationship to the vice president for academic affairs should be changed. It may be more appropriate to report to the vice president for student affairs. The political antics of administration are centered on perceptions of power, not ability. The perception was that the position was too powerful for an African American woman with a reputation for getting things done, but it was expected of the Anglo male who preceded me.

Barbara once worked as a dean at an elite research one university on the East Coast. Her insight brings to the surface some of the underlying, unspoken assumptions found in traditionally white university environments.

I was dean of a large college at a predominantly white university. The statement "I was a dean" means, of course, that I am not a dean any longer. Why is that? Were they not pleased to have a black woman take on the helm of a complex mess and have her straighten it out? Indeed! They were proud to say, "An African American woman is the dean of our college." It was a glorious affirmation! And, I might add, an affirmation that carried with it some degree of pride, albeit not the kind of pride that says, "We got us a black one, and WE got her BEFORE university X got one!" It's only now, looking back on the situation, that I can draw such conclusions. I did not reflect on my hiring at the time as I have described it above. No, not at all. I came to the university with the very best credentials and experience. In fact, I was perfect for the job. But perfection was not what they were seeking. Ability did matter to some extent, but the important thing, I think, was to hire a minority person—a capable minority person. In my position, I thought I enjoyed the same privileges and

> perks of my colleague deans, but what a surprise lay ahead for me. Being a woman leaves you out of the club—being a black woman closes the door to the club. Why? Because after the door had opened, the question would be: What do you want? (not spoken: What do you want? Well, you got the damn job—now what do you want?)

Even though Carla's credentials were superior to those who preceded her, colleagues questioned her ability to effectively perform her administrative responsibilities. As she noted clearly, the person to whom she should report was very important. The notion of power and privilege implies whiteness and/or maleness (whichever is applicable). It is not about administrative competence, but power and privilege.

Carla and Barbara assumed their positions with a level of pride and a strong sense of self-worth. However, their ability to perform effectively in administrative positions seems to have been questioned by their colleagues. Even though Carla maintained her position and Barbara did not, their ability to effectively fulfill their positions was hampered by their colleagues' perception of them.

Gloria is now an associate professor at an East Coast Ivy League institution. She narrates her views of positions held:

> I was a 25-year-old assistant professor when I first became a faculty member at a predominantly white institution in the Deep South. Some of the older "good old boys" thought I was a graduate student, although I was their colleague. One in particular could not even remember that I was his colleague and would not allow me to attend a dissertation proposal defense because he "thought I was a graduate student!" When the other colleagues told him I was the new faculty member, his face turned red as he apologized for his behavior. Interestingly, he later became one of my biggest supporters.

While the above experience is memorable, Gloria further describes her colleagues' perception of her as exhibited in their daily behaviors:

> Most of my colleagues were convinced that I would be unable to fulfill my responsibilities as a faculty member after the first year. Well, how wrong was their perception? I was able to move a course on racial and ethnic minorities from ten or twenty students to thirty–plus students each semester; the class eventually grew into two sections. I also wrote research proposals that were well funded. This resulted in my being published in refereed journals, just like a few others did. My career took off on a fast track, and I had no problems getting tenured and was promoted a few years later.

Madelyn, who has held positions as both a faculty member and an administrator, presently holds a distinguished endowed chair at a university in the Northwest. According to Madelyn:

> This is a mixed bag . . . with both upheavals and downheavals. There have been many positive acknowledgments of my competence and efficiency both as a faculty member and administrator. In fact, I received the highest award that the institution bestows for someone who has exerted unusual influence on the life of the institution.

As an associate professor, Madelyn was in a department of eight white males, five of whom were full professors. Three faculty members in the department were white female assistant professors. She continues:

> My downheaval period occurred during my transition from associate to full professor. A primary source of irritation is related to importance placed on awards, publications in nonwhite journals, and participation in majority-dominated professional organizations. When white folks receive awards from white organizations and constituencies, the awards are considered important and prestigious. When we receive a distinguished award from a black professional organization or a national leadership position, no real importance is given to the award or position, even though it is earned based on the work for which we were

> hired. White folks receive an award of a dead or dying discipline and it is lauded. Publications in white "mainstream" journals are praised, while much work that is not associated with these outlets is considered inferior or less scholarly.

After several months of figuratively fighting with the five white male full professors who were to vote for or against her promotion, Madelyn received full professorship. Gloria and Madelyn shared the same assumed expectations of failure on the part of white colleagues. Yet they were able to emotionally overcome those negative expectations and succeed in reaching the goals to which they aspired. The cases of these two African American professors lend credence to the notion that despite how scholarly our work may be, it is always in question by white colleagues.

Another theme suggested by some of these prominent African American women in academia was, "Exceed the expectations." The views of one scholar, Darlene, are excerpted below:

> Since you're black you've got to do more and be better, to prove acceptable, was the number one guideline on the script inside my head of things Mom and Dad recommended for survival and success. Yet, here I am filing a controversial lawsuit against a major statewide university because much to that university system's surprise and woe, I believed and actually practiced my parents' guiding principles. Now, it seems that a federal court judge and jury will determine if Mom and Dad's nurturing provided me a deciding advantage or set me up for a cruel letdown.

Robin, in the transition from assistant to associate professorship, writes:

> If I could isolate the behaviors and thoughts that I contributed to the situation surrounding my professorship experience, my story would be easier to tell. In other words, it can be assumed that another woman (any other woman) under the same environmental conditions would have a different story to tell. After

> successfully defending my dissertation, I took an assistant professor position in a land grant institution in the Northeast. As a new doctoral recipient, my head was in the clouds. Unlike many of my European American colleagues (learned during the years), I had little or no understanding of the roles and actual responsibilities of a professor, other than observations made during my undergraduate and graduate training. I soon discovered, however, that performing the traditional responsibilities of research, teaching, and service was much less disconcerting than appraising and appropriately coping with stresses and demands that would appear suddenly and often without previous warning. I mean that it was not difficult for me to excel in all three areas, given my ability to perform successfully in most professional pursuits. However, the stress came when I was so frequently compared to white colleagues, some of whom were not even up for tenure and promotion. Somehow my assertiveness, work ethic, and authenticity enabled me to exceed the criteria for the transition from assistant to associate professor. I live by the theme: Exceed the expectations in order to be identified as equal . . . or even superior—the latter of which is the case for some of us when comparisons are made.

Connie's response to the question parallels that of Darlene and Robin. She states:

> I was in awe of the perception others apparently had of me. It seemed to me that the expectations were pretty low and when I simply did my job with what I considered normal competency, I was lauded beyond my imagination. It has always been important to me to do well and fulfill my responsibilities, but either my supervisors were not accustomed to blacks doing a fine job in general or to anyone doing well in the positions held. Anything beyond and above receives most often just verbal acknowledgment, but does not translate into new and greater responsibilities or opportunities I desire. Now, it's something of the ilk, "Well, gee thanks very much, but I will be passing out goodies

for jobs well done to white-male-come-lately faculty who need to make a name for themselves."

Having to exceed expectations in order to prove acceptable was yet another challenge faced by Darlene, Robin, and Connie. Typically, an African American female faculty person or administrator has to outperform others (whites) just to maintain perceived equal performance status with them. It is ironic that when we outperform our colleagues, there are still ways in which some of them can discount our performance.

The dedication of African American women to their work is not always rewarded with equal measure. In fact, despite continuous efforts to surpass the expectations of others, promotion into the administrative realm of higher education is the exception, not the norm. Doris, an administrator in the Midwest, writes:

> What are the possibilities for African American women in terms of administration? On the surface, there seems to be an array of positions available and opportunities to move up the administrative ladder, but only for those in student services and support positions that are peripheral to the academic units. At this university, there are numerous black women who "assist" others in middle management and even some upper-level management positions. But you do not see African American deans and vice presidents emerging from the faculty ranks to become academic administrators. Now you will say, "But you did it." Yes, I did it, but I must have been a blip on the screen, a fluke, an anomaly.

The sobering reality is that Doris's words ring true. Her successes—and the achievements of other African American women of administrative-level status—are not representative of the majority of African American women in academia. What is interesting about Doris's story is that she, like many other African American women in the academy, is in an area with low power, low pay, and low prestige, a position such as student affairs. This type of position does not affect the nature and substance of what students learn—these positions only provide services, of a nonacademic nature, to students. The holders of these positions are always the helpers, not the leaders (similar to a nurse/doctor relationship). Many African American women who do not enter administration find that they have not escaped the challenges previously faced.

Mildred, who is an associate dean of student affairs at a private college in the Midwest, reflects on her experiences prior to defending her Ph.D. dissertation:

> I had very difficult early experiences related to "others'" perceptions of my ability to perform my duties as an administrator. I could share many examples . . . but the one that had the most profound impact on me was when I worked in the Michigan area at a branch campus of a major university. I was working within the office of admissions and was having a conversation with a member of the faculty (white woman) about the status of minority admissions and my recommendations as they related to both recruitment and retention at the university. The conversation, in my opinion, was not a difficult or contentious one, rather just a sharing of thoughts. Her response to me was something like, "You can't say anything to me until you get your Ph.D." I was so shocked at the comment and at the anger and disgust expressed by this woman that I was speechless. All I could think after that encounter was, just wait, I'll be back, and THEN we'll talk! And to this day, I look forward to the opportunity to speak with her again, now as her peer, to remind her of what she said and thank her for the motivating challenge to my authority. The negative turned into a positive out of the arrogance on the part of that white woman, who thought she knew more about the "minority" experience than I did as an African American woman and a graduate of that institution.

Mildred continues describing her general views of the present academic environment:

> I also find that I am interrupted more frequently in meetings, that my points are dismissed more readily, and that these behav-

iors are exhibited, unfortunately, by men and women equally. Although I have been employed at both public and private, large, medium, and small research one and two institutions in more than one state, I still have to prove I am competent. I also still must prove that I have an understanding of what student affairs is all about. On the contrary, I have colleagues who have not earned their doctoral degrees and who have not worked anywhere other than their current location. They have never been challenged; their competence is assumed, and they need to prove nothing. Finally, and peculiarly enough, I am often asked questions about my personal life related to my sexuality and sexual activity. Folks seem very interested in what I do on weekends and whom I am doing it with. They almost interview the men that I have invited to join me at various campus events, asking them where they live, how long they have known me, and if they will be staying the weekend. This is not behavior I see happening to anyone else.

Dorothy, a professor at an east coast university, discusses her colleagues' perceptions of her in her work environment:

There is an assumption that African American women are stupid, crazy, or both. As an administrator, some colleagues tried to block work I was doing at a given time. I was close to becoming the dean of graduate education at this university when white colleagues appeared to have become uncomfortable around me. On numerous occasions, white colleagues would paraphrase what I'd said as if I am not capable of expressing myself. Once I said, "Pardon me, but I think I can speak English well enough." It is patronizing behavior that diminishes status and serves as a constant expression of our being underestimated. In various battles over status on campus, I have managed to win—often by virtue of being underestimated. It becomes a backward weapon when people think you are stupid or crazy, and they almost think that you can't do anything. I was able to ignore certain things

> and wage my fight for whatever I had in mind. I did become dean of graduate education, despite the odds.

There is the recurring theme of the restating of African American women's comments by white colleagues, sometimes even claiming the ideas as their own. Having to prove competence is also a recurring theme. And for Dorothy, whites' inquires into her personal weekend activities imply a racism that suggests that African Americans are more interested in sex than academics. Both Mildred and Dorothy expressed their feelings of being "underestimated." Colleagues spoke on their behalf without invitation to do so, and often their contributions were dismissed. The cases of Mildred and Dorothy represent the experience of many African American women administrators: Even though their superior work spoke for their competence, they still found their abilities questioned by less qualified colleagues.

Patricia is now a full professor at a university in the South. Here she reflects on the general views of the positions she has held:

> In my early experiences and even today, I find I must prove myself. In my early experiences, I would volunteer for responsible roles, apply for positions, and would not be given an opportunity. On one occasion, I was successful in my application, interviewed well with the review committee, and had my name forwarded to an administrative position, and the hiring administrator chose another person because he had a "gut feeling" that the other person would be better for the job. The other person was a blonde, white female.

Marsha, who is an associate professor at a research two university in the Midwest, describes her previous experiences in an administrative position as follows:

> I believe there was a significant number of individuals who supported my move into an administrative position. There was, however, a small minority who didn't. These individuals never supported anything that was sponsored on the campus by Afri-

can Americans. When students protested against the discriminatory practices in the university, they would often apologize for the students' behavior to the administration. They were the individuals who lobbied with white racist administrators to reduce faculty positions and the budget of the African American studies department in 1985—even though they were faculty in African American studies. I never took them seriously. But the administrators evidently did. They did little publishing and hardly ever participated in academic symposiums, conferences, and workshops. They were promoted to administrative positions. Against the wishes of the faculty, the dean appointed one of them as the acting chair of our department. Oh—and by the way, that person was a white male with a doctorate degree in community leadership.

The common thread between Patricia and Marsha is that despite their fulfillment of required criteria, neither applicant got the administrative position. The solidity of racial attitudes indicates the inability of many white Americans to recognize the continuous racial discrimination faced by African American women in academia. The catch-all in Patricia's case was the administrator's "gut feeling" that another person would be better for the job. Apparently, in these situations, credentials matter little and the decision about who does or does not get the job is relegated to subjective interpretations. Given the fact neither of the women got the jobs for which she interviewed signals that when all things are relatively equal, African American women come up short.

OUR VOICES ABOUT OUR EXPERIENCES OF RACISM IN THE ACADEMIC ENVIRONMENT

Racial oppression by whites and blacks' response to that oppression are key elements in our discussion of the life worlds of African American women in the United States. (St. Jean and Feagin, 1998, p. 11)

This part of the data analysis "provides" cases where African American women are responding to the issue of racism as a specific variable in their academic environments. They have provided narratives in response to: Your experiences of racism on the part of your assumed superiors, i.e., chairperson, dean, students, etc.

Shirley, a recently tenured associate professor at a very reputable research one university on the west coast, writes:

> My white colleagues seem to view my overall existence through the eyes of white women daily. I find this to be particularly true in developing course offerings. There tends to be a strong emphasis on courses in gender, which my white female colleagues push for and get. However, as the only woman of color in my department, I find less concern for courses which focus on race and ethnicity. There is only one course which has such a focus, and it has been taught by the same white male for the past fourteen years. I have submitted a proposal for a course on women of color on two different occasions, and [received] a response from the curriculum committee to "revise and resubmit." As a matter of fact, some of the same suggestions for revising the proposal have been made, yet the same suggestions keep coming up.

In Shirley's narrative, we may observe that whites view African American women's existence (sense of self) through their contacts with white women. However, existing research refutes that assumption (Myers, 1980; 1991):

> It may not be so obvious, but it is equally true that as Black women, separated in space but belonging to the same social category (race, sex, and in some case, age) we have come to recognize our common fate. Thus, we may deal with the effects of racism in a somewhat uniform manner. (Myers, 1991, p. 21)

We may also observe that the same assumption exists in course offerings. More emphasis is placed on courses in gender than on courses in race and ethnicity. This pattern occurs at colleges and universities throughout the nation.

Marie, who was an untenured assistant professor, directed a research grant within her discipline. She describes her experiences of racism as follows:

> I have found even those who try to be politically correct are not really aware when they are racist. When my colleagues try to use me as the spokesperson for the entire African American society—they don't know how racist they are. Or, when the discussion is about diversity, and I'm finally chosen to serve on a committee—that's racism. When the West Virginia jokes run wild—that's racism. When the new white faculty are mentored—that's racism. When recommendations for minority students are needed and they ask only the minority faculty—that's racism. When your responses are interpreted—that's racism. When others are asked what you mean—that's racism. When I accepted an administrative position, my associate director sent the comment to that department that the staff would not be able to work with me because I was loud. When an anonymous letter surfaced with the statement, "Only a black would show such loud behavior"—that's racism.

According to Jackie, a tenured full professor at a research two university in the southwest:

> There were few blatant acts of racism. I think most were aware that I had little tolerance for such and acted accordingly. The acts came in the form of questioning my abilities for tenure and promotion after having been given the guidelines and following them. Certainly, I could not have accomplished all of this alone. "How much of this did I do on my own?" was generally the question raised when I served as a collaborator on projects. In the face of questions, I continued to have enough projects and activities so that I could be successful in at least one.

Helen, an untenured assistant professor at a midwestern university, notes:

> In spite of my previous statewide oversight of a multimillion dollar budget, the management of a several thousand dollar program budget was questioned by an individual without budgetary management experience. In lieu of granting a travel budget, the number of trips was specified, which resulted in excess program costs. Some colleagues made comments about their experiences with African Americans and inferred that unethical behavior was learned from these interactions.

Marie's, Jackie's, and Helen's statements of racist experiences have a recurring theme: Their intellectual ability and level of performance are constantly questioned by white Americans. In addition, verbal abuse, stereotypical perceptions, and "outright racist practices" prevail in their everyday life experiences in white academia.

In response to this question regarding African American women's experiences of racism on the part of superiors, Peggy, an assistant who served in a tenure track position at a research two university in the northeast, writes:

> I have been excluded from committees and denied resources all under the guise of seniority. I can identify clear-cut cases of variant rules governing me and my activities, all with negative or punitive impact. Opportunities are denied in a way in which the budget or deadlines are conveniently pointed to me as the culprit. I have had per diem reduced after a professional trip and the budget for it had been approved. I have had openly hostile remarks made to me by colleagues and students.

Sheila, a recent Ph.D., assumed an assistant professor tenure track position at an elite small private college in the east. She shares her experiences as follows:

> My former department chair asked a fellow search committee member (after my campus visit) if he didn't think I'd be "eaten

> alive" by students in my proposed area. I am usually fairly well accepted by whites because of my demeanor (unaffected, seemingly friendly), my appearance (usually quite conservative), and my speech ("quite white," I've been told). Interestingly, though, I'm usually viewed as somehow weak, although I have done everything they had me to do and I'm still sane. I have had my department chair tell me on several occasions that I must do things that my colleagues do not have to do, i.e., post office hours and turn in travel reimbursements before the due date.

In Peggy's case, hostility and disrespect from both colleagues and students come into focus. Sheila's case spotlights male dominance and gender oppression.

Faye is an assistant professor at a university where the chief administrators publicly stress the need for more representation from African American scholars. She writes:

> I was assigned to teach a course in sociocultural studies to undergraduates. I was advised that this course was considered to be a joke by many of the students. This particular course was designed to create an appreciation of cultural diversity for undergraduates, while a majority of the instructors for this course were African American. I wondered what this meant. Was it that many other white males and females in the department did not think that this course was really significant? It is obvious that the department's curriculum manifests a dominant Caucasian ideology and that the voices of Caucasians are privileged. I am aware of professors making statements such as, "Students are complaining that they do not understand your assignments and that you talk to them in condescending ways because you are black." Complaints made by students tend to be more numerous in regards to African American instructors and professors. The department chair usually favors the students in such complaints. In one case, a student was disrespectful to an African American professor, and the professor was admonished rather than the student.

Joyce, an assistant professor of African American studies who was up for tenure and promotion the next year, writes:

> Moreover, you are too African, or just beat the race issue to death, if you try to deal with racist remarks made by certain white students toward you in the classroom. You are supposed to accept the fact that white students should be free to say such things as, "I pay your salary so you will teach what I say." I believe that some students would like for the professor to rewrite the history of racial or ethnic oppression instead of stating the facts printed in texts. The message is clear—if it's black, it cannot be worthy of academic consideration.

The voices of Faye and Joyce hold a common thread in terms of their experiences as departmental representatives on committees and/or classes related to race, ethnicity, or multicultural issues. While some African American female faculty may have a special interest in these areas, it can also work to their detriment. These experiences illustrate the lack of importance assigned to issues of race, ethnicity, and multiculturalism by students, colleagues, and administrators. The assignment of racial and ethnicity-related activities to any African American female faculty member can result in the addition of these as permanent responsibilities (along with, not in place of, her other academic assignments).

The time commitment and value of involvement in such activities often go unrecognized and unappreciated by colleagues. The lack of validation for racial, ethnic, and cultural activities for African American female faculty member's efforts not only go unrecognized but are also punished by a promotion and tenure process that stresses research productivity (Phelps, 1995, p. 259).

Laura, a full professor at a research two university in the mid south, discusses her experiences with students and notes:

> I have been the subject of a student newspaper article attack. I was denounced for the viewpoints I voiced about the lack of diversity within the staff of the paper and the content of the paper.

> The president of the university urged colleagues to "give no attention to me." In connection with this incident, a group of white males overtook and taunted me as I walked between buildings one afternoon. I have had a student go so far as to write in a journal assignment derogatory remarks such as "The professor is a loser." Final course papers have been removed/stolen from the dropoff box outside my door as colleagues have chided that "kids play these kind of pranks, you're making too much of it." Students have openly and directly insulted me during class sessions and even attempted to initiate mutinous efforts as I stood before them. Others have disrespectfully sought to carry on conversations during my lectures and there have been attempts to intimidate by physically rushing me in groups demanding grade changes at the conclusion of a course meeting. The sad thing is that in a career of more than fifteen years, I have observed that the pursuit of an "A" has become a frenzy for white students as they interact with me.

Laura further states that recently she asked four other (white) faculty persons if they had observed the students' "A" frenzy. Their response was, "No, they seem to accept the scores they have made."

According to Stella, who was up for tenure and promotion to associate professor at a north central university:

> My experiences with racism have centered on students. I teach medical students, and frequently some have voiced concern about blacks being genetically inferior. Student evaluations go like this: "Why does she have to talk about race all the time? This is not a class on race. She is unfair or biased. She never explains anything. She is never around to answer questions or provide help. She is totally unqualified to teach."

It is important to note that sixteen of the African American female professors received student evaluations with the statement, "She is unqualified to teach! Fire her!" Others listed comments on student evaluations such as "I have never had a black teacher before coming to this university. So why must I have to take her class?" "I wanted a class at 10 that was a convenient time. But, why does she have to be teaching it?" "I like the course and she seems to know her stuff . . . but I just don't like her." "She is such a black bitch." Note*:* A few of the respondents noted having been called a "black bitch" to their face and in student evaluations.

Close similarities may be observed among these women's early experiences and how they were perceived by others, especially students, in their ability to fulfill their responsibilities as faculty member or administrator. Judgments of character and merit are imposed not only by colleagues. African American women may find that students are also threatening factors in the road to tenure. Students' sense of privilege and hostility have a negative effect on the careers of African American women who teach them (Daufin, 1995, p. 35). Daufin shares some of her experience in an article published in *Black Issues in Higher Education.* She admits that she has tried "every teaching method, device, approach and strategy, short of stripping and bribery," to achieve higher numeric teaching evaluations. "But none of it works," she writes. Relative to the issue of student/professor interaction in teaching about racism and sexism, Daufin's article lends support to the narratives given by the respondents for this research. She concludes:

> As a womanist professor, I don't know how I may avoid addressing the race and gender issues that anger so many students. Students who complain about having to think about race and gender issues in a class of mine that is not specifically about women or people of color always suffer from acute perceptual distortion. . . . For instance, in a newswriting class that meets 20 to 30 times, I will address racist and sexist language in one or two classes, as written in the syllabus. Yet, complaining students wail that I harped on race and gender issues in a class where they didn't think that they should have to hear about it at all. (Daufin, 1995, p. 35)

She suggests that if students require a course title to warn them that they may have to think about how white women and people of color fit into the subject area, we should change all catalogue course titles to specify that the course will deal only with the world view of white males, such as "Writing News about White Men" or "White Males in Literature 101" (p. 35). In reality, harsh judgment prevails in determining our pursuits of successful outcomes in academe.

It is believed that tenure brings power, privilege, and prestige (Burgess, 1997). Thus, the single most important goal that most faculty members have upon entering the academy is the attainment of this status, which is often difficult and sometimes impossible but always highly desirable because it ensures job security, more money, eligibility leaves, and institutional support for research (Burgess, 1997, p. 227).

Frequent references were made in my survey to experiences of racism in the respondents' efforts to secure tenure and promotion. Rose states:

> The most poignant experience with faculty was that of tenure and promotion. When I came up for tenure and promotion, I had eight articles in print and six forthcoming. The vote for tenure was tied, and my chair cast the deciding vote against me. There was so much dissension in the ranks that it was decided that the department committee would take a second vote at the end of the year. On the average, senior faculty whites were promoted with two articles or one book (either edited or authored). However, I was told that some of my articles were in African American journals and did not "meet the expected standard." In response to the six articles that were forthcoming, I was told that many journals are going out of print; therefore, the committee "has no guarantee" that any of my articles would make it to print.

By the end of the year, all of Rose's six remaining articles were published—making a total of 14 articles—and she was "reluctantly" granted promotion and tenure. She notes:

> This marked the largest number of publications ever reported for tenure and promotion. The result of their action was that for six years thereafter, no one who came up for tenure (all white) was able to reach the level imposed upon me. Their response to

> my question concerning the great disparity in quantity vs. quality of articles accepted was that "their standards had been raised prior to my going up, and most had made it through just before my time."

Are they making the rules as they go along, depending on the person who is up for tenure and promotion? You be the judge on that one. Similarly, Beverly describes her experiences of racism in securing tenure and promotion:

> My tenure experience perhaps most clearly crystallizes the complex interaction of race and gender on my campus. I was the first. In 1995, my fourth year there, I submitted a case that had unqualified backing from the department and the dean. The campus ad hoc committee, in its wisdom, felt that tenure could not be granted right away. The latter, which was retained, indicated that my case was excellent and worthy of tenure. No additional documentation was required. However, the rank of associate and the actual status of tenure would be deferred for a year. No reason was given for the decision to defer, and when my dean made inquiries through channels, he was told that it was "too soon" for me to receive tenure. I should mention that my publication record exceeded that of some full professors (white males) and many associate professors (males).

Yet Kathy states:

> Most of the professors at my university are tenured by publishing at least five articles. However, I was not given the opportunity to come in as a tenured professor, even though I had published fifteen articles in top journals. This proves the point that blacks must be twice as good as whites to receive the basics. Blacks are devalued in this society. It hurts most white people to acknowledge the intellectual skills of people of color.

Being the only African American woman in the division of the social sciences, Stacy, an instructor at a community college, writes:

> One particular problem that seems to prevail is the class loads that one may have. I have noticed through the years that my classes are overloaded with students. There are a limited number of students that were allowed to enroll in a class. The usual number is between twenty-five and thirty-five students. However, I have had thirty-nine to forty-five students in my classes. The students were allowed to register and enroll in the classes, without my permission. My colleagues would have fifteen to twenty-five students. Even in the summer school sessions, I would have a class of twenty-five or more and maybe my colleagues would have ten to fifteen students. Therefore, instead of making two classes out of my larger classes, I would end with a payment for one class, and they would be paid for two classes of ten to fifteen students.

From the preceding cases, we find examples of differential standards, demeaning of scholarship, and profound institutional racism. Promotion and tenure are significant events in every professor's career. For those of us who are particularly susceptible to the sometimes subtle biases that accompany race and/or gender, the process can be fraught with peculiarities.

OUR VOICES ABOUT OUR EXPERIENCES OF SEXISM IN THE ACADEMIC ENVIRONMENT

It is believed that sexism directly shapes and determines relations of power in our private lives, in familiar social spaces, and certainly in the academic arena. It is fair to assume that sexism and sexist oppression are real issues in our lives as African American women.

For this part of the data analysis, narratives were requested for addressing issue 3: Your experiences of sexism on the part of your assumed superior, i.e., chairperson, dean, students, etc. I must inform the reader that very few African American women in the sample provided much discussion of actual experiences of sexism in white academia but stated that it does exist in their academic environment. Therefore, I am including those who gave specific experiences first.

Mary writes about her experiences of sexism on the part of her chair:

> As a woman with a very young baby returning to work after a maternity leave, I asked the chair (white male) to schedule my classes after 9 a.m. He said that he "could not make special allowances for me because I was a woman." I was assigned an 8 a.m. class on Mondays, Wednesdays, and Fridays.

She goes on:

> Later that year, our chair (the same man who rejected my request for later classes) was going through a divorce and his term had expired. Although most of the all-white faculty—two women and two men—had voiced how "unfair and vicious" the chair had been, they voted for him to serve another term as chair. The reason they gave for their decision was that he could not stand another rejection from his colleagues after the rejection of his divorce. Of course, I was the lone protester and fighter against gender inequality.

Melanie's response to the issue of sexism was as follows:

> Many of my colleagues pretend that they have not experienced or seen any prejudices shown on this campus. I often laugh and move quickly to complete my work and continue taking care of my responsibilities. I was placed on many committees when I first arrived here twenty years ago. One particular committee I will never agree to serve on again—the social committee. I was given the responsibility to set up, serve, and clean up before, during, and after the business meetings. I was never able to attend the business meetings because I was always in the kitchen. I resigned after a full year of being the perfect hostess and the best kitchen helper available. It is assumed the women will clean the coffee section, arrange the meetings, take notes, and do all arrangements for visitors—that's sexism.

Clear in Mary's case is the fact that a male's emotional response to rejection via divorce is more important that a woman's concern for spending time with her young baby. And his colleagues agreed that he should be given the privilege that Mary was denied. Talk about sexism!

Melanie's narrative depicts the "mammy" image that has evolved to a more contemporary form. That image continues to impact the lives of many African American women, including those who occupy professional positions on predominantly white college and university campuses (Hoke, 1997, p. 296). Regardless of our educational attainment, we are still perceived as nuturant domestic servants by most white Americans.

OUR VOICES ON THE COMBINED EXPERIENCES OF RACISM AND SEXISM

Hoke (1997) asks the question: Is it race or is it sex? (p. 294). Benjamin (1991) responds to the question based on her research that even those who attempt to distinguish between sexism and racism by looking "at the language, the underlying assumptions and consequences" still conclude "that sometimes the situation is confounded by a combination of both racial and sexual components, making the distinction extremely difficult" (p. 177).

The African American women in the sample were asked to respond to the following question: Which of the two practices (racism or sexism) would you say had the greatest effect on you? Please explain why you chose this practice. Included here are direct responses given as written by each individual African American faculty person or administrator in a traditionally white college or university:

- Racism has had the greatest effect on me. My colleagues are constantly silent on matters of racism in contrast to matters of gender and sexuality. Issues relevant to my success as a black female are minimized, and the politics of the department indicate that I am in a fish bowl in terms of my race.
- Racism is far greater than sexism. I don't think the world sees African American women as women, so they don't necessarily address

the issue of gender with me. I have always sought a global view of both so that I am informed about both and can function in both spheres, because I belong in both and cannot separate the two. I have used it consistently as a source and a skill because few people expect you to have knowledge of both areas; they respond as if you only know one perspective.

- Even though I know both negative behaviors and practices are the result of immoral, self-diminishing feeling, racism for me was more destructive. The issue for me has been race. I believe that race is the more provocative agent of maltreatment for women of color. Skin color and racial and ethnic identifiers, in my belief, incite biased and discriminatory behavior more readily. This seems to be tied to our national cultural experience.
- Most definitely, racism has affected me most. I am never surprised anymore as to the extent to which institutions of higher education value diversity . . . that is, until it looks different.
- Racism has had the greatest effect on me because it is easier to identify. The men seem to think they are being "gentlemen" when they perform sexist acts.
- Racism had the greatest effect on me. In my opinion as a black female, sexism is a secondary concern. As a black faculty member on a white college campus, you are constantly reminded that you are black at "our" school.
- Both racism and sexism played a part in affecting my job experiences. It was truly a combination of both, with race as the "driving" force.
- I assume that most white people react to my race more than they do my sex, but I could be wrong. However, I believe this is because I have to prove myself in situations with white women. White women are invariably assumed to be smarter and better. For example, I was in a situation where I did considerable work on a project to help a white woman with her research. Her work was chosen over mine, even though my input was the basis for what she submitted.

- In response to which of the practices (racism or sexism) has had the greatest effect on me—without a doubt, it is racism. Reared in a forced racially segregated world, racial attitudes shaped the very essence of my being. I had to find a philosophy of life that allowed me to feel good about myself and the world, without internalizing the stigma of inferiority. Sexism, on the other hand, has never been a serious issue for me, though I am aware of gender differences and discrimination. My position is and has been that the positive and negative factors of gender differences built into the social fabric cancel each other out. As I see it, prior to the last movement, the society had built-in rules to protect the woman's status and roles as interdependent on that of the man's status and roles. The workforce rules were my only bone of contention.
- Sexism, undoubtedly, has occurred but I see race/sex as combined or race as the primary factor influencing responses to me. It was a real challenge to be the first black female at a faculty/administrative level in a historically Southern white male-dominated institution in the Deep South in 1971.
- In the past, sexism has not been as problematic as has been racism. It is evident but not overwhelming—I am in no way minimizing. While it is difficult to prove racism within the race, it occurs. As an African American woman, I have experienced racism from white men and women as well as African American men and women. Race is an issue. Neither racism nor sexism deters me from accomplishing my goals; though they are unnecessary hindrances. However, I view it as a challenge and stay positive.

Having noted that racism has the greatest effect on her, this respondent notes:

- Here I have always commanded my space and was confident enough in my abilities that being woman did not matter as much as being a black woman. A female colleague once told me that I was not "feminist enough." And I didn't understand the struggles that women had to face in academia. Ironically, it was clear to me that at least they were in academia! On occasion, I do have to remind my supervisor that I am, in fact, a woman as well as an African American. This comes on the assumption that I would not be interested in women's issues because I am African American, as if women's issues are just for the "other" women. I take that with a grain of salt and press forward with my agenda of success.

Other responses included:

- Racism by far had greater effect on me than sexism and can be counted on from both men and women on campus. I think, in general, black women as faculty members do not count as women, but as black people in general.
- Racism by far has had a greater effect on my career and on me as a person. Perhaps it is because there have always been women in my department to share or provide support in terms of sexist attitudes or practices. But I am the only woman of color to challenge the issue of racism.
- I don't think that race can ever be secondary in a historically white institution. But the combination of race and gender is doubly deadly in a historically Southern white male-dominated institution. Both black men and females of whatever color were perceived as lesser individuals as compared to white men.

In terms of whether sexism affected them more than racism, only four of the African American women in my sample noted sexism as having affected them equally to racism and two noted sexism as affecting them more. Their comments indicated sexism to be very subtle, including preferential treatment of African American males in hiring to key positions and African American males' insensitivity to the sexism that exists. Following are some examples:

- Sexism has affected me most. African American males were consistently promoted to administrative positions for minority "representation," so that their voices would be heard.
- In general, I feel that sexism is more oppressive than racism on my campus, but both are problematic. In fact, the complex interaction

of racism and sexism is much more detrimental than either evil operating independently. In particular, African American males and females are not especially united on my campus due, I believe, to the relative privilege that the men enjoy. They are quite insensitive to the sexism that exists.

- While both racism and sexism are forever present, sexism appears to be the dominant factor during this period of my life.
- Sexism is much more subtle and indirect. It is experienced more often in a group context or collectively. I have perceived no clear-cut issues here. I once received a "humorous" response to the mention of scholarly pursuit in collaboration with two white female faculty members by reducing the significance of the activity and referring to the authors as "you and the girls."

On the issue of which (racism or sexism) had the greatest effect on them, the majority of the respondents cited racism, while a few cited sexism. However, two of the African American women suggested some difficulty in determining which of the two factors had the most effect on them. Consequently, each implied that both racism and sexism may be perceived as of equal effect.

According to Phyllis:

> I would submit that it is difficult to distinguish one from the other as it related to which of the two has had the greatest impact on me both personally and professionally. First, let me share that as an African American woman . . . I was taught as a child that being female was less of a challenge to my quality of life experiences than being "black." I come from a family of very strong African American women, and so not only received this message verbally, but also internalized it based upon the examples that were set by the women on both sides of my family. This attitude, however, was real in many ways like a double-edged sword for me as I developed and grew in my gender consciousness. While I was sensitive to the challenges that existed because of my race, and could quickly and easily identify present and potential dangers, I

> rushed into many situations feeling that they were relatively "safe" locations racially, and encountered challenges that I had not anticipated based upon my gender. As the consciousness level has risen, and as I too have risen professionally, I can look back on previous positions held in higher educational administration and say with confidence that being a woman is more of an issue now that I am in a leadership position than it was when I occupied entry and midlevel administrative positions. So, in answer to the first part of the original question, I would submit that race and gender have impacted upon my experiences equally, with race functioning more as a challenge in the beginning of my career—gender functioning more as an issue now!

Cynthia, who titles her comments "Gender matters—is it possible to unravel the African American female essence?" writes:

> In most instances, I predict that the word "woman" is used to refer to white women and the word "black" is used to refer to black men. Somehow the essence of being both black and a woman seems to get lost. It is as if one's identity can be divided or compartmentalized. . . . I can never talk of being "only black," nor can I speak in any genuine way about being "only female" because I find it impossible to hold one constant while I examine the other. In my mind, it is the transactional and interconnectedness relationship within the selves of African American women that makes our stories so unique. In short, we have the capacity to see the world through both sets of eyes and also the ability to experience the joy and pain offered in relation to mistreatment because of sexism and racism (i.e., double jeopardy). Therefore, I must admit that I am affected by both racism and sexism equally in the white academic environment.

In view of Phyllis's response, experiences of both racism and sexism affected her at different periods of her life. Even though she was socialized early in life that her gender would be "less of a challenge to her quality of life than her race," sexism became of great importance in her academic environment. Therefore, she concluded that she is affected equally by both racism and sexism. Cynthia also suggests difficulties in determining which of the two affected her the most. Hence, she noted that she was affected by racism and sexism equally.

THE RESULTS

The results of the research show that numerous African American women in the sample reported that their qualifications are continuously challenged in their academic environments. Some noted that often their ideas are viewed as legitimate only when white colleagues state them as their own. Frequently noted by most of the respondents was that they were subjected to magnified and extreme evaluations by their colleagues. In addition, feeling pressured to outperform other (white) colleagues just to maintain perceived equal performance status with them was stated by a large number of the women.

Several of the African American faculty members also noted that research topics that focus on race were not considered of much importance, especially in the tenure and promotion process. It was shown that even when their research was published in journals dedicated to such a focus, the journals were not considered to be prestigious or reputable enough.

A number of the respondents addressed faculty/student interaction as an issue in the academic environment. This included harsh judgment relative to teaching style and disrespect for course content especially when race is discussed. Some even noted outright verbal and nonverbal attacks by students. The majority of the women reported that racial experiences are typically far more overwhelming sources of oppression than gender experiences.

7

Coping with Indelible Experiences

A primary source of stress among African American women faculty and administrators in traditionally white colleges and universities is derived from their experiences of racism and sexism within their work environment. The victims of racism and sexism are stressed by unrelenting oppression and discrimination (Pierce, 1995). It is Pierce's belief that

> oppression and discrimination are distributed on an individual and group basis. It may be overt or covert, acute or chronic, mental or physical. It varies in intended seriousness from lethal to hatred to subclinical amusement. For the victim, depending on perceptions and circumstances, the stress may seem omnipresent and ubiquitous. It is therefore common for many, if not most, victims of racism and sexism to believe at some time that their lives are in danger, because of actual or threatened terrorizing and torture from the oppressor. (1995, p. 277)

In continuing his discussion of stress derived from racism and sexism, Pierce identifies some inherent operational prejudices that are institutionalized and widely applied and that produce and sustain stress in the victim. First, in investigating racism, he offers three of the most pernicious of these variations:

1. Almost always in academic studies, the dominating agent uses the submissive agent as the target to be understood, helped, analyzed, categorized, altered, and controlled. Hardly ever is the dominator the subject of study by the dominated. Almost never in academic studies is the viewpoint of the submissive agent sought. If it is sought or considered, there is frequently a conscious or unconscious presumption that is trivial, irrelevant, and marginal or even immature, miniature, and worthless. Almost exclusively the dominant agent serves as gatekeeper and arbiter of what is published or taught, as well as when, where, and how it is published or taught.
2. Inherent difficulties must be acknowledged in terms of both sexism and racism, of which women are the victims. The difficulties are found commonly in any dominant/submissive pattern, such as coach/player, parent/child, teacher/student, white/black, male/female, employer/employee relationship, or any situation rife with terror and grief.
3. Four fundamental questions must be addressed in any submission/dominance engagement: Can both the oppressed and the oppressor be happy and content at the same time? When, why, where, and how much does the oppressed resist victimization versus when, where, and how much does the oppressed accommodate oppression? How does the oppressed differentiate when a dominant agent's actions and/or words represent an individual viewpoint versus when they represent a collective viewpoint? Where there seems to be some degree of acceptance or validation, how does the oppressed recognize when this acceptance indicates being wanted or welcomed versus when it indicates being merely tolerated or needed? (Pierce, 1995, p. 279)

Pierce's very clear interpretation of the stress resulting from experiences of racism and sexism is relevant to this research. However, a discussion of how we cope with these experiences is also important.

Over the last years (1973 to the present), I have been researching and writing about self-esteem and coping among African Americans in general and African American women specifically. I define coping as alternative ways of dealing with the pressures of society. Hence, coping helps us to provide some explanation of the resources used by African American women in adjusting to the various social pressures we experience in everyday life. This is to say that there is a causal relationship between what we think of ourselves and coping. Feelings of self-worth lead to a greater ability to cope (Myers, 1980; 1984; 1991; 1998).

If we know who we are and what we are about, we should know fairly well how we deal with unpleasant experiences. This simply means "tapping our inner resources." After this, we develop and maintain an image of ourselves, despite adverse experiences (Myers, 1991, p. 22). It has been proven that numerous African American women at various levels of employment appear to retain a remarkable sense of self-worth (e.g., Dill, 1988; Rollins, 1985; Collins, 1989). It is through the power of self-definition that we as African American women intellectuals have long explored this private, hidden space of our consciousness that allows us to cope with and, in most cases, transcend the confines of race, class, and gender oppression (Collins, 1989, pp. 92–93).

I chose not to include any questions about self-esteem and coping for this book. However, it is very interesting that several of the respondents referred to these concepts as they addressed how they deal with experiences of adversity in academe. For example, Rolanda wrote:

> It is believed that my general outlook on life not only colors my perceptions of my experiences in the workplace but also colors how my superiors and colleagues think of and relate to me. I am told that I approach life as "a detached onlooker" rather than as "an active participant," meaning that I have the ability to be involved and yet maintain a certain distance. In all probability, this attitude (approach) towards life and work was developed as a result of my beliefs about living in a society that presumed me to be inferior by reason of race. To this extent, it appears that I de-

> veloped an "inner-directed" philosophy of life to regulate and control my behaviors, which enables me to have a positive sense of self. Therefore, I approach my work as a job more so than as a career. This attitude allows me to focus on doing the best work that I can do without a great deal of "self-esteem" investment.

Another respondent expressed her feelings in dealing with her experiences. According to Wanda:

> My experiences have made me tremble with anger, heightened my distrust, and tested my perseverance. But I never allowed the situation to destroy my hope and alter my dreams. Why? Simply because I know who I am and what I am about, and I will never allow any acts of racism, sexism, or any other-isms to destroy my sense of who I am or destroy my level of competence in academe or any other facet of my life.

One respondent discusses her personal experiences and how they have helped her cope with racism:

> I really believe that having gone to a historically black college for my undergraduate degree contributed greatly to my ability to deal with my experiences of racism in traditionally white institutions where I received my Ph.D. and where I am presently employed. Why do I say this? Simply because my sense of who I am was reaffirmed in that early environment prior to going into traditionally white environments.

In her narrative titled "Trying to Fit In," one of the African American respondents gives her take on our experiences as follows:

> Alienation, social dislocation, political and psychological bankruptcy are descriptors of what I felt while teaching at two predominantly white colleges. While the outcomes were different, the experiences were as psychologically damaging. This made healing a slow process, which for some African American women is never complete, while for others we slowly regain our center.

Truer words were never spoken. Yes, we do regain "our center." If we were not able to regain our center, the few of us would not have remained in traditionally white institutions throughout the nation. For years, it has been my belief that our key to coping with racism and sexism as African American women is to get an image of ourselves based on how well we do whatever we are doing and on how others whose opinions matter to us view our successes.

My previous research shows that our social support systems serve the primary function of developing and maintaining a positive level of self-esteem. One of the African American women's narratives complements the notion of special support systems. She writes:

> My family experiences provided the strength to compete in a white racist academic environment. My father always told me that I could be anything I wanted to be. However, he admonished that whites would try to block my progress. In addition, a strong church participation helped to buffer the effects of racism. I was raised in a close knit church that encouraged my intellectual pursuits.

Some of the women made specific reference to their early socialization in terms of a sense of "self." What do I mean by "social support systems"? I define social support systems as those helping agents or individuals within their environment whom African American women identify as providing social support and feedback in solving problems or during periods of crisis. Please refer to the illustration following. We may observe from the following diagram that close friends and family are of equal importance for African American women. I can certainly relate to this because I often find myself touching bases with my significant others through whatever forms of communication necessary. It has been proven that close friends are more supportive of emotional feelings, values, and beliefs. In society at large, some people tend to discuss problems only with personal friends rather than family members. This, again, is a way of coping with otherwise unbearable life situations (Myers, 1991, p. 28).

Diagram
Social Support Systems in Development and Maintenance of Self-Esteem

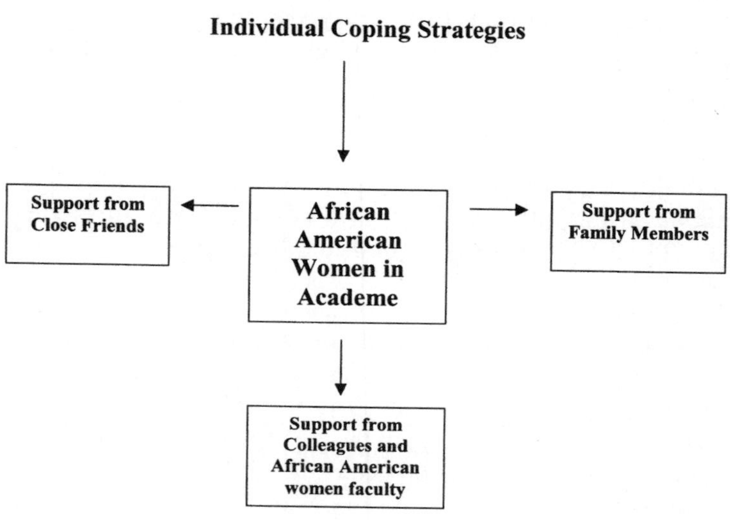

Our self-worth and self-reliance must be internally generated, and support networks must be established both in and out of academic settings. This process is forever present as we interact with our significant others throughout life. We tend to maintain a steady pace by holding on to external and internal support systems in the face of adversity. It may not be so obvious, but it is equally true that as African American women separated in space but belonging to the same social category (race, sex, class, and, in some cases, age), we have come to recognize our common fate. Thus, we may deal with the effects of racism and sexism in a somewhat uniform manner (Myers, 1991). As W.E.B. Du Bois puts it:

> No other woman on earth could have emerged from the hell of force and temptation which once engulfed and still surrounds Black women in American with half the modesty and womanliness they retain. (1969)

This is not to imply that African American women in traditionally white institutions are "superwomen" in terms of physical strength. Coping is not to be interpreted as being hardened to the effects of adversity. We are certainly vulnerable to being moved by such things as sorrow, loneliness, neglect, unhappiness, and even happiness. But we are also capable of finding the means and alternatives for developing and maintaining our emotional stability in terms of a positive sense of self. However, our positive sense of self does not erase the negative effects of racism and sexism that we experience in our everyday lives in traditionally white colleges and universities. It only makes it a little bit easier to deal with.

In a truly just society, both racism and sexism and any other type of "-ism" should be eradicated. Moving toward the successful inclusion of women and minorities involves commitment and action by institutional leadership. Institutional leaders can show commitment to the advancement of African American women in many ways. Possibilities include highlighting the excellent work of individual African American women faculty, placing the participation and success of minority women high on the list of critical issues to the institution, and recruiting qualified African American women for significant positions within the administration. Other faculty should be educated about the needs of African American faculty and be committed to making noticeable change. It is not enough simply to tolerate diversity. Instead, it should be accepted and embraced. In the journey toward tenure or other promotions as well as long-term job satisfaction, it is most important that African American women maintain self-confidence—because this is what will help transform predominantly white institutions.

The stories have been told and undoubtedly their tellers have known a range of human experiences unknown by most. The frustration of reaching endlessly can be exhausting to the African American woman who captures victory after victory—only to tell herself to push harder. She knows that the respect she so desperately seeks, as an African American and as a woman, is not likely to find its way past the rigidity of an environment defined by someone else.

Many women experience differential treatment not only because of race but because of gender as well. For African American women, this subordinate status twice defined is very pronounced in academe.

This sample of African American women in traditionally white colleges and universities reported general experiences that were significantly influenced by racism and sexism. In many ways, these African American women were not given credit for outstanding work efforts and achievements. Whether through exclusion, through behavior based on prevailing stereotypes, or through blatant skepticism about their professional ability, colleagues directly and indirectly acted to undermine the success of the African American women sampled in the research for this book.

Such influence is by no means undetected in the everyday struggles of African American women in academia. However, of one thing nearly all respondents are certain: The racism and sexism that work to hinder African American women are largely unnoticed by others. The continual fight for change is a lonely battle for many, at times fueled only by an incredible fortitude. Such profound inner strength rests at the heart and soul of women who refuse to wear labels—especially the label that calls them victim.

> Perhaps in the future the realities of African American women in academia will be significantly brighter. It will be through joint efforts of academic institutions as a whole and through the dedication of determined individuals that today's realities will be replaced by new revolutions in thought and action. Reality is not infinite and unchangeable; rather, it has the potential to be shaped by a society that embraces diversity. In the end, reality will be what we want it to be. And for African American women in academia, this reality will be a promising indicator of their outstanding accomplishments—past, present, and future. (Myers, 2000, p. 22)

The future? Yes, the future lies in the hands of the next generation of African American women in the academy. Representation of that generation is found in young *Djanna A. Hill*, who wrote the Epilogue that follows.

Epilogue

In offering an epilogue to this book, I turn our attention to the title, *A Broken Silence: Voices of African American Women in the Academy.* In this text, Dr. Myers shares with other black women a space in which their stories can be told in the way they experience those stories. Little effort has been made in the past for black women to narrate their experiences. The stories in *Voices* pierce the academy with truth-telling examples of the racism and sexism that exist in academe as well as in society at large. In this text, Dr. Myers attempts to answer many questions, yet most significantly answered is the question as to why there are so few black women faculty in higher-education institutions.

We are well aware of the early successes of outstanding female teachers. Black women have a special calling to teach. Yet, the progress of black women in the higher ranks of university faculty has been painfully slow. While women comprise approximately 34.6 percent of all faculty in American higher-education institutions (Hill, 1999), research indicates that black women represent only 3.2 percent of full-time faculty at institutions of higher education in this country (Gregory, 1999). Black women who teach in the academy are often found at historically black colleges and universities (Berry, 1982; Collier-Thomas, 1982; Gregory, 1999). At predominately white research institutions, fewer than 4.7 percent of the faculty in higher education are black, and less than 2.2 percent are black women (Atwater, 1995a, 1995b; Cartledge, Gardner, and Tillman, 1995).

As Dr. Myers makes strikingly clear, given the double discrimination of racism and sexism that black women continually experience in the academy, there can be little doubt why they are not equally or well represented throughout the full spectrum of institutions of higher education. Racist and sexist encounters that black women faculty experience include instances where their intelligence has been questioned by both colleagues and students, times when their teaching decisions, course content, and research interests have been challenged, and cases when they have been advised wrongly by mentors who stereotype black women into low-performing and powerless positions. These experiences are not unlikely in an environment that has been traditionally a "white male club." Since the academy was established and is (mostly) maintained by the dominant majority (Maitland, 1990), rules pertaining to appointment, retention, promotion, and tenure, for example, are driven predominately by white male norms, values, and standards.

As we synthesize the stories told here, we find that some black women find it difficult to have the issue of sexism treated as a legitimate topic by colleagues. Black women professors report racist and sexist treatment received from white men and white women who seem unable to deal with a black woman in a position of authority. More so, black women professors share feelings of isolation and of being ignored and passed over for promotion in favor of less qualified people. Kawewe (1997) reminds us that misconceptions and stereotypes about race and sex lead to treatment of and interaction with black women as a label, mystifying the real person behind a stigma and encouraging self-fulfilling prophecies by the dominant sex and race that hold power.

> Because hiring, promotion, and retention are based on the perceptions of those hiring, there has been a tendency for those de-

> cisions and judgements to be made on the basis of homogeneous production, which excludes women, African Americans, Native Americans and other special populations. (Kawewe, 1997, p. 263)

When thinking of merely existing in academe under the kind of atmosphere that negates your presence as a black person and as a woman, there is little doubt why black female professors are underrepresented in higher-education institutions.

Dr. Myers's path-breaking book contributes to the conversation about the experiences of black women and adds richness to the existing research on black women in the academy. Within the bulk of studies on African Americans in education, little attention seems given to the roles women faculty play, and even less has considered the impact of race and gender on those roles. In light of what little is studied, researched, and written about regarding black women professors, a study of this nature is not only timely but also significant. Indeed, documenting the experiences of black women in the academy as her story, in the way she experiences, perceives, and narrates, is invigorating. Dr. Myers and this research give me, as well as other young black women entering the academic professorate, encouragement. Reading rich descriptions of the experiences of those who came before us only enhances our preparation. We need more books like this one. More stories need to be documented. After reading *Voices*, I felt not alone in my quest for racial uplifting, in my personal encounters with racism and sexism, and in my isolation of being one of the few black women in my doctoral program. Documenting our experiences and being well informed of others' encounters help to establish our own norms and standards.

As we have read, it seems as if we are ill represented in the academy because of issues relating to race and gender. Yet, now that we have heard these stories, what will we do about the racist and sexist practices that exist in the academy as well as in society at large? What policies should we promote? What programs should be initiated? Herein lie our next steps. We must continue the conversation.

Djanna A. Hill

Appendix

RESEARCH INSTRUMENT

Lena Wright Myers
Professor of Sociology
Ohio University
Athens, Ohio 45701

(740) 593–1375 (office) or (740) 593–1350 (department)
e-mail: myersle@ohiou.edu

Dear Colleague:

I am in the process of completing a manuscript about African American women in traditionally white colleges and universities (both faculty and administrators in all disciplines). I am reviewing the realities of our experiences primarily from the structural/functionalist and the conflict perspectives, respectively.

Complete anonymity for this manuscript is secured both legally and professionally, unless you suggest differently. Only you will be able to identify your comments qualitatively, once the book is released. Therefore, I have systematically selected you among the numerous distinguished female faculty/administrators in traditionally white colleges and universities in the U.S. for this research pursuit. I welcome your response to your experiences in both past and present positions. Your anonymous responses will be included in a chapter entitled: Our Voices about Our Experiences. Our voices need to be heard! I am asking you to please respond in narrative form to the following general issues where applicable:

1. Early experiences relative to how the persons with whom you work perceive your ability to fulfill your responsibilities as faculty/administrator.
2. Your experiences of racism on the part of your assumed superior, i.e., chairperson, dean, students, etc.
3. Your experiences of sexism on the part of your assumed superior, i.e., chairperson, dean, students, etc.
4. Which of the two practices (racism or sexism) would you say had the greatest effect on you. Please explain why you chose this practice.
5. What is your present rank at the college/university where you are presently employed?

Please respond via e-mail or regular mail to the addresses given above. It is important to note that pseudonyms are used for the respondents to assure confidentiality.

References

Atwater, M. (1995a). African American female faculty at predominately white research universities: Routes to success and empowerment. *Innovative Higher Education*, 19(4), 237–240.

Atwater, M. (1995b). Administrative support in initiating transformations: A perspective of an African American female. *Innovative Higher Education*, 19(4), 277–285.

Banks, W. (1984). Afro-American scholar in the university. *American Behavioral Scientist*, 27, 325–338.

Benjamin, L. (1991). *The black elite: Facing the color line in the twilight of the twentieth century*. Chicago: Nelson-Hall.

Benokraitis, N., and Feagin, J. (1986). *Modern sexism: Blatant, subtle, and covert discrimination*. Englewood Cliffs: Prentice Hall.

Berger, P. (1973). *Invitation to sociology: A humanistic perspective*. New York: Overlook Press.

Berry, M. (1982). Twentieth century black women in education. *Journal of Negro Education*, 51(3), 288–300.

Bey, T. (1995). African American females and academe: Power and self- development. *Innovative Higher Education*, 19(4), 287–295.

Billingsley, A. (1992). *Climbing Jacob's ladder: The enduring legacy of African American families*. New York: Simon and Schuster.

Blackwell, J. (1983). *Networking and mentoring: A study of cross-generational experiences of black graduates and professional schools.* Atlanta: Southern Educational Foundation.

Blackwell, J. (1989). Mentoring: An action strategy for increasing minority faculty. *Academe*, 6, September/October, 8–14.

Blackwell, J. (1991). *The black community: Diversity and unity.* New York: HarperCollins.

Blauner, R. (1972). *Racial oppression in America.* New York: Harper and Row.

Blum, D. (1988). Black woman scholar at Emory University loses 3 year battle to overturn tenure denial, but vows to fight on. *Chronicle of Higher Education*, 22(A), 15.

Blumer, R. (1972). *Racial oppression in America.* New York: Harper and Row.

Bower, B. (1996). The social power of African American female administrators in the community college. *Community College Journal of Research and Practice*, 20, 243–251.

Bowie, M. (1995). African American female faculty at large research universities: Their need for information. *Innovative Higher Education*, 19(4), 269–276.

Braxton, B. (1973). *Women, sex, and race: A realistic view of sexism and racism.* Washington, D.C.: Verta Press.

Brewer, R. M. (1988). Black women in poverty: Some comments on female-headed families. *Signs: Journal of Women in Culture and Society*, 13, 331–339.

Brittan, A., and Maynard, M. (1984). *Sexism, racism and oppression.* New York: Basil Blackwell.

Brown, S. (1988). *Increasing minority faculty: an elusive goal.* Princeton: Educational Testing Service.

Brown, V. (1998). African American women faculty and administrators: Surviving the multiple barriers of discrimination. *Multicultural Campus*, 169–187.

Burgess, N. (1997). Tenure and promotion among African American women in the academy. In Benjamin, L. (ed.), *Black women in the academy: Promises and perils.* Gainesville: University of Florida Press, 227–234.

Carter, D., Pearson, C., and Shavlik, D. (1988). Double jeopardy: Women of color in higher education. *Educational Record*, 68–69, 98–103.

Carthy, L. (1992). *Black women in academia: A statement from the periphery.* In Himani Bannergi, et al. (eds.), Boston: South End Press.

Cartledge, G., Gardner III, R., and Tillman, L. (1995). African Americans in higher education special education: Issues in recruitment and retention. *TESE*, 18(3), 166–178.

Christiansen, M. D., Macagno-Shang, L., Staley, K. H., Stamler, V. L., and Johnson, M. (1989). Perceptions of the work environment and implications for women's career choice: A survey of university faculty women. *Career Development Quarterly*. 38, 57–64.

Civil Rights Act of 1964 (codified as amended at 42 U.S. c.-2000e to 2000e-17.) 1982.

Collier-Thomas, B. (1982). The impact of black women in education: A historical overview. *Journal of Negro Education*, 51(3), 173–180.

Collins, P. (1989). *Black feminist thought: Knowledge, consciousness, and the politics of empowerment.* New York: Routledge.

Collison, M. (1999). Race women stepping forward. *Black Issues in Higher Education*, 16(7), 30–31.

Corbett, E. (1992). The shame of current standards for promotion and tenure. *Journal of Advanced Composition*, 12(1), 111–116.

Curry, B. R. (1995). Racism and sexism: Twenty-first century challenges for feminists. In Bell, L. A., and Blumenfeld, D. (eds.), *Overcoming racism and sexism*, (19–21). Lanham, MD: Rowman and Littlefeld.

Daufin, E. (1995). Confessions of a womanist professor. *Black Issues in Higher Education*, 12, 34–35.

Defour, D., and Hirsch, B. (1990). The adaptation of black graduate students: A social network approach. *American Journal of Social Psychology*, 18, 487–503.

Dill, B. T. (1988). Making your job good yourself. Domestic service and the construction of personal dignity. In Barkman, A., and Morgan, S. (eds.), *Women and the politics of empowerment* (pp. 33–52). Philadelphia: Temple University Press.

Du Bois, W.E.B. (1961). *The souls of black folks.* Greenwich, CT: Fawcett.

Du Bois, W.E.B. (1967). *The Philadelphia negro.* New York: Shocken.

Du Bois, W.E.B. (1969). *Dark waters.* NY: AMS Press, 186.

Du Bois, W.E.B. (1993). The race for inclusion. In James, J., and Farmer, R. (eds.), *Spirit, space and survival*: African American women in (white) academe. New York: Routledge.

Edwards, J., and Camblin, L. (1998). Assorted adaptations by African American administrators. *Women in Higher Education*, 7(11), 33.

Epps, E. (1989). Academic culture and the minority professor. *Academe*, 36(5), 23–26.

Essed, P. (1991). *Understanding everyday racism: An interdisciplinary theory.* Newbury Park: Sage.

Exum, W. (1983). Climbing the crystal stairs: Values, affirmative action, and minority faculty. *Social Problems*, 30(4), 382–399.

Exum, W., and Menges, R. (1983). Barriers to the progress of women and minority faculty. *Journal of Higher Education*, 54(2), 123–144.

Farmer, R., and James, J. (eds.). (1993). Spirit, space, and survival: African American women in (white) academe. New York: Routledge.

Fields, C. (1996). A moral dilemma. *Black Issues in Higher Education*, 13(17), 22–29.

Franklin, C. W., Jr., and [Walum] Richardson, L. (1972). Toward a paradigm of substructural relations: An application to sex and race in the United States. *Phylon*, 33. 242–253.

Greenburg, M. (1995). Considering tenure–it's not hold writ: Can we talk? *Educational Record*, 76(4), 35.

Gregory, S. (1999). *Black women in the academy: The secrets to success and achievement.* New York: University Press of America.

Grillo, T., and Wildman, S. M. (1996). Obscuring the importance of race: The implication of making comparisons between racism and sexism (or other isms). In Wildman, S. M. (ed.), *Privilege revealed.* New York: New York University Press.

Guillaumin, C. (1995). *Racism, sexism, power and ideology.* New York: Routledge.

Harvey, J. (1989). *Some thoughts on organizational backstabbing: Or, how come every time I get stabbed in the back my fingerprints are on the knife?* San Francisco: Jossey-Bass.

Hill, D. (1999). Distribution of faculty by full- or part-time status, tenure status, and gender. *Black Issues in Higher Education*, 16(1) March 4.

Hoke, B. (1997). Women's colleges: the intersection of race, class and gender. In Benjamin, L. (ed.), *Black women in the academy: Promises and perils* (pp. 291–301). Gainesville: University of Florida Press.

Holland, G. (1989). *The recruitment, retention and promotion of African American faculty in the U.S.* (ERIC document reproduction service no. ED 349 918).

Hooks, B. (1981). *Ain't I a woman? Black woman and feminism.* Boston: South End Press.

Hooks, B. (1989). *Talking back: Thinking feminist, thinking black.* Boston: South End Press.

Howard-Vital, M. (1989). *African American women and mentoring.* (ERIC document reproduction service no. ED 360 425).

Johnson-Bailey, J. (1994). *Making a way out of no way: An analysis of the educational narratives of reentry black women with an emphasis on issues of race, gender, class, and color.* Unpublished doctoral dissertation, University of Georgia, Athens, Georgia.

Johnson-Bailey, J. (1999). The ties that bind and the shackles that separate: Race, gender, class, and color in a research process. *Qualitative Studies in Education*, 12(6), 659–670.

Kawewe, S. (1997). Black women in diverse academic settings: Gender and racial crimes of commission and omission in academia. In Benjamin, L. (ed.), *Black women in the academy: promises and perils* (pp. 263–269). Tampa: University Press of Florida.

King, D. (1992). Unraveling fabric, missing the beat: Class and gender in Afro-American social issues. *Black Scholar*, 22(3), 36–43.

Krenshaw, K. W. (1989). Demarginalizing the intersection of race and sex: A black feminist critique and antidiscrimination doctrine, feminist theory and antiracist politics. *University of Chicago Legal Forum*, 140–143.

Lagowski, J. J. (1992). The compatibility of teaching and research. *Journal of Chemical Education*, 69(8), 115–149.

Lichtenberg, J. (1998). Racism in the head, racism in the world. In N. Zack, et al. (eds.), *Race, class, gender and sexuality: The big question.* Malden, MA: Blackwell.

Lindsay, B. (1994). African American women and brown: A lingering twilight or emerging dawn? *Journal of Negro Education*, 63(3), 430–442.

Lindsay, B. (1997). Surviving the middle passage: The absent legacy of African American women education deans. *Minority Voice in Educational Reform*, 3–32.

Lorde, A. (1984). *Sister outsider.* Trumanserg, NY: Crossing Press.

Lorde, A. (1998). Age, class, and sex: Women redefining difference. In Rothenberg, P. S., (ed.), *Race, class, and gender in the United States: An integrated study.* New York: St. Martin Press.

Maitland, C. (1990). The inequitable treatment of women faculty in higher education. In Welch, L., (ed.), *Women in higher education: Changes and challenges* (pp. 246–254). New York: Praeger.

Malveaux, J. (1999). Replicating ourselves in the 20th century and 21st centuries. *Black Issues in Higher Education*, 16(22)–23.

Marable, M. (2001). *Race, class and gender in the United States.* New York: Worth.

McGuire, G., and Reskin, B. (1994). Authority hierarchies at work: The impacts of race and sex. *Gender and Society*, 7(4), 487–506.

Morgan, G. (1986). *Images of organization.* Beverly Hills: Sage.

Moses, Y. (1989). *Black women in academe: Issues and strategies.* Washington, D.C.: Association of American Colleges, Project on Status and Education of Women. (ERIC document reproduction service no. ED 311 817).

Myers L. W. (1975). Black women and self-esteem. In Millman, M., and Kanter, R. (eds.), *Another voice: Feminist perspectives on social life and social science.* Garden City, NY: Anchor/Doubleday.

Myers, L. W. (1980). *Black women: Do they cope better?* Englewood Cliffs: Prentice Hall.

Myers, L. W. (1998). *Black male socialization: Revisited in the minds of respondents.* Stamford, CT: JAI Press.

Myers, L. W. (1991). *Black women, Do they cope better?* (Rev. ed.). New York: Edwin Mellen Research University Press.

Myers, L. W. (2000). Realities in academe for African American women. *Journal of Women in Higher Education,* 9(4), 21–22.

Myrdal, G. (1994). *An American dilemma: The Negro problem and modern democracy.* New York: Harper.

North, J. (1991). Strangers in a strange land: Women in higher education administration. *Initiatives,* 54(2), 43–53.

Palmer, S. (1983). In the fishbowl: When blacks work in predominantly white colleges. *Chronicle of Higher Education,* 10(17) September, 14.

Phelps, R. (1995). What's in a number? Implications for African American female faculty at predominantly white colleges and universities. *Innovative Higher Education,* 19(4), 255–268.

Phillip, M. (1993). Tenure trap: Number of obstacles stand in way of tenure for women. *Black Issues in Higher Education,* 10(17), 42–44.

Pierce, C. M. (1995). Stress analogies of racism and sexism: Terrorism, torture and disaster. In Willie, C. V., Reikor, P., Kramer, B., and Brown, B. (eds.), *Mental health, racism, and sexism.* Pittsburgh: University of Pittsburgh Press.

Pleck, J. H. (1993). Men's power with women, other men, and society. In Cyrus, V. (ed.), *Experiencing race, class, and gender in the United States.* Mountain View, CA: Mayfield.

Powell, L. C. (1983). Macho and black feminism. In Smith, B. (ed.), *Homegirls: A black feminist anthology.* New York: Kitchen Table—Women of Color Press.

Richardson, L. (1988). *The dynamics of sex and gender: A sociological perspective.* New York: HarperCollins.

Ries, P., and Stone, A. J. (1992). *The American women: A status report.* New York: W. W. Norton.

Rollins, J. (1985). *Between women: Domestics and their employers.* Philadelphia: Temple University Press.

Romero, M., and Margolis, E. (2000). Integrating sociology: Observation on race and gender relations in sociology graduate programs. *Race and Society,* 2(1), 1–24.

Rothenberg, P. S. (2001). *Race, class and gender in the United States* (5th ed). New York: Worth.

Ryan, W. (1998). Blaming the victim. In Aquirre, A., and Baker, D. (eds.), *Sources: Notable selections in race and ethnicity.* Guilford, CT: Dushkin/McGraw-Hill.

Scala, A. H. (1994). *Race, gender and academia. Off Our Backs*, 24(4), 7.

Scales-Trent, J. S. (1989). Black women and the constitution: Finding our place, asserting our rights. *Harvard Civil Rights–Civil Liberties Law Review*, 10–12.

Slevin, K., and Wingrove, C. (1998). *From stumbling blocks to stepping stones: The life experiences of fifty professional African American women.* New York: New York University Press.

Smith, F., and Zorn, T. (1981). Educational equity. Presented at the American Educational Research Association Conference, Los Angeles.

Smith P. (2000). A menage to sapphire and her sisters' in academia. *Women in Higher Education*, 9(2), 31.

Smith, P. R. (1991). Separate identities: Black women, work and Title III. *Harvard Women's Law Journal*, 14, 22–31.

Sorcinelli, M., and Austin, A. (1992). *Developing new and junior faculty.* San Francisco: Jossey-Bass.

Sorcinelli, M., and Billings, A. (1992). *Developing new and junior faculty.* San Francisco: Jossey-Bass.

Staples, R. (1984). Racial ideology and intellectual racism: blacks in academia. *Black Scholar*, 15(2), 2–17.

Stein, N. (1998). Affirmative action and the persistence of racism. In Aquirre, A., and Baker, D. (eds.), *Sources: Notable selections in race and ethnicity.* Guilford, CT: Duskin/McGraw-Hall.

St. Jean, Y., and Feagin, J. (1998). *Double burden: Black women and every day racism.* Armonk, NY: M. E. Sharpe.

Tatum, B. D. (2001). Defining racism: "Can we talk?" In Rothenberg, P. (ed.), *Race, class, and gender in the United States: An integrated study.* New York: Worth.

Thomas, M. (2000). Anything but race: The social science retreat from racism. *African American Research Perspective*, winter, 80.

Thomas, W. I., and Znaniecki, F. (1927). *The Polish peasant in Europe and America* (2nd ed.). New York: Alfred A. Knopf.

Wildman, S. (1996). *Privilege revealed: How invisible preference undermines America.* New York: New York University Press.

Wilkinson, D. (1991). The segmented labor market and African American women from 1890–1960: A social history interpretation. *Research on Race and Ethnic Relations*, 6, 85–104.

Wilkinson, D. Y. (1998). Gender and social inequality: The prevailing significance of race. *Journal of the Academy of Arts and Sciences*, 24(1), 169.

Wilkinson, D. (2000). Rethinking the concept of "minority": Task of social scientists and practitioners. *Journal of Sociology and Social Welfare*, 17(1), 115.

Williams-Green, A., and Singh, K. R. (1995). Differences in perceptions of African American women and men faculty and administrators. *Journal of Negro Education*, 64(4), 401–408.

Wilson, R. (1993). Why the shortage of black professors? *Journal of Blacks in Higher Education*, Fall, 25–34.

Womble, M. (1995). Transition from a teaching institution to a research institution: An African American female perspective. *Innovative Higher Education*, 19(4), 241–253.

Yanick, S. J., and Feagin, J. (1998). *Double burden: Black women and everyday racism.* Armonk, NY: M. E. Sharpe.

Zack, N. (1998). *Race, class, gender and sexuality: The big questions.* Malden, MA: Blackwell.

Zuckerman, H. (1992). The careers of men and women scientists: A review of current research. In Zuckerman, H., Cale, J., and Bruer, J. (eds.), *The outer circle: Women in the scientific community* (pp. 27–56). New York: Norton.

Index

About the Author

LENA WRIGHT MYERS is Professor of Sociology at Ohio University and the author of numerous scholarly contributions to sociology, race, ethnicity, class, and gender.